Tongues

Tongues

multilingual multicultural magazine

Issue #1 ————————— June 2015

Tongues Issue #1 —— June 2015

Founder & Editor-in-Chief —— Raelke Grimmer
Senior Editor —— Elise López
Sales and Marketing Manager —— Adam Troyn
Design, Layout and Typesetting —— Ondrej Klos and Nikola Giacintova

Published by Tongues Press.
This project has been assisted by the South Australian Government through Carclew.

Tongues Press
136 Cashel St, St Marys
South Australia, 5042
Australia
www.tongues.com.au
editor@tongues.com.au

Tongues

Government
of South Australia.

Tongues acknowledges that the land on which this magazine was created is the traditional country of the Kaurna people of the Adelaide plains. We recognise and respect their cultural heritage, beliefs and relationship with the land.

Contents

A Note from the Editor

Two years ago, I had the idea of creating a multilingual and multicultural magazine, which would celebrate the world's linguistic and cultural diversity. Language is an integral part of culture as culture is an integral part of language, and the two cannot be separated out. I imagined a magazine where different languages would be celebrated as a crucial aspect of celebrating different cultures. A place where people of all linguistic and cultural backgrounds could share their stories and their expertise, in their languages.

One year on from this initial idea, I launched Tongues as an online magazine, with the support of Express Media through the 2013 Young Writers' Innovation Prize.

Now, one year since the launch of the online magazine, the very first print edition of Tongues is here, thanks to the support of the South Australian Government through Carclew. Within these pages, you will find written pieces about diverse languages and cultures. Some articles are written in English only, others appear in foreign languages alongside their English translations. Even if you only understand the English, I encourage you to take the time to look at the pages in foreign languages. Get a sense for the way the language appears on the page, the characters which are different from your own alphabet and imagine that language as holding the key to that community's culture.

In this issue, you'll read about Montréal, a city caught between two languages. You'll discover the influences which have shaped the Polish language, a community in the Barossa Valley in the process of reclaiming their heritage language and the experience of being a young woman living in Morocco. You'll find an interview with writer and asylum seeker case worker Mark Isaacs, and another with Professor Ghil'ad Zuckermann, Chair of Linguistics at the University of Adelaide, who is working with the Barngarla people of South Australia is an effort to revive the Barngarla language. Within these pages you'll find articles in Bavarian, English, French, German, Indonesian, Polish and Spanish.

The writing within this first edition has been contributed by amazing writers from all over the world. You may notice differences in the Standard English used by different writers. These differences have been maintained to respect the native or learned Standard English of each individual writer. Tongues is here to give a voice to speakers of languages other than English, and to explore the amazing linguistic and cultural diversity which exists on our planet. Language is part of our identity as humans, and all tongues deserve to be heard.

Raelke Grimmer——Founder and Editor-in-Chief

On Montréal, Language, and Being Free

By Joel Mak

Joel Mak is an Australian writer living in Montréal. His short stories and poems have appeared in ARNA as well as Cuttings. He also writes about music for Aphramag, Semplesize, and Montreal Rampage.

Last summer I had the pleasure of biking daily from my house to Montréal's *Grande bibliothèque*, the biggest hub of the *Bibliothèque et archives nationales du Québec*, on the corner of *boulevard De Maisonneuve* and *rue Berri.* The boulevard is named after the founder of the city, Paul Chomedey de Maisonneuve. It is unclear who or what *Berri* is named after, though most *Montréalais* cyclers know it for the hill it swells into between *rue Ontario* and *rue Cherrier*, with short respite through the tunnel under *rue Sherbrooke*; motor-powered traffic zooming past, as your glutes and hamstrings strain to power a bicycle.

My ride started in the Plateau district, opposite a *dépanneur*, the Québécois word for convenience store, colloquially shortened to *dep*, which originates from the old French verb '*dépanner*', meaning to lend a hand. Through Parc Lafontaine, tourists took pictures of squirrels that sketched cute arcs as they hopped in the grass. Teenagers in rock band tees tried wilder parabolas with their skateboards, while others occupied different degrees on the idle to over-exertion spectrum of physical activities. On hot days, I saw people lounging on the park slopes in beach attire, muscled bodies going through HIIT routines, soccer players chasing mis-kicked balls, old *pétanque* players laughing and singing along to classic *Québécois* rock tunes on their boom boxes.

My destination's contemporary glassy façade, when compared to its neighbor the brown neo-gothic Judith Jasmin Pavilion of the *Université du Québec à Montréal* (UQAM), looks like the more accomplished child who went abroad for studies and came back with a cool haircut. Both of these buildings are part of the *Quartier latin*, a salad bowl of diversity *par excellence*. Here classes, languages, and lifestyles meet and bounce off each other like hockey players in a ring. Backpackers, blue collars, and affluent couples all descend from the appropriately numbered 747 buses

By Joel Mak

On Montréal, Language,
and Being Free

that shuttle to and from the airport. They are greeted by a panoply of UQAM students, street buskers, and *itinerants* selling copies of *'L'Itinéraire'*[1].

With or without permission, shirtless punks and hitchhikers wiped down car windscreens at red lights. Drivers either spared change, or received a big fat *tabarnak*[2] and/or mucus-ridden spit. On the same street corner, charity workers and Hare Krishna devotees chattered up those who hadn't already cut a wide berth around people they saw approaching with a mouth-open smile, gigantic wave, and clipboard. They competed for attention with the homeless who were prepared to tell you about their life in both French and English, for a quarter or two.

To live in Montréal is to be constantly bemused, especially if one cares in the slightest for the history of Québec. Why is a major artery *(rue Ontario)* named after a province that is easier to make fun of than to visit? Why is a street *(rue Sherbrooke*[3]*)* named after the British North American Governor General of 1816-1818? Why does no one bat an eyelid when a Crown corporation is named the National library of Québec, *de jure* a province like any other?

The answers satisfy any dilettante historian or trivia enthusiast. *Rue Ontario* isn't named after the province but the Great Lake. John Coape Sherbrooke got along well with Louis-Joseph Papineau[4], the leader of the 18th century Patriotes who sought

---

1   Québec's 'Big Issue'.

2   A swear word literally translated to 'tabernacle', i.e. a dwelling place for divine presence documented in the Old Testament. Québec's severed relationship with Catholicism has resulted in scrolls' worth of blasphemous words used in everyday life.

3   Also the name of the sixth-largest city in Québec, about an hour and a half east of Montréal.

4   Papineau lends his name to an avenue and metro station, not to mention the fact that most people don't have a clue who Sherbrooke is.

democratic reform and autonomy for Lower Canada's (present-day Québec) political institutions[5]. Lastly but perhaps more contentiously, most Québécois identify themselves as Québécois first and Canadian second. This type of banal, as opposed to xenophobic, war-mongering, border-building nationalism is the norm in Québec. It is why you see more fleurdelisés than unifoliés flags; why Canada Day is Québec's Moving Day and on this day nobody is nonplussed when a separatist procession is led by a ponytailed man sitting on a trailer bandstand towed by a ute, strumming sad state-of-the-nation songs; why the Journée nationale des patriotes is celebrated as the Queen's birthday in the rest of Canada.

It takes only four paragraphs before Wikipedia's entry on Québec brings up the independence debate. Québec has had two referendums already. The last one in 1995 saw the indépendantistes lose out by less than a percentage point. If there's anything Québec lacks, an intellectual culture focused on teasing out all the particularities of Québec's national question is not it. Today, some Québécois want independence, more don't, and quite a lot are tired of talking about it. Case closed?

Unlike Toronto, mining cities in the west, or the Whistler slopes, Montréal sees a small share of Australian expatriates. There's a Café Melbourne owned by Melbournites[6], a pie shop whose smartly abbreviated name is TA (for *tourtière australienne*) that nobody gets, and a Facebook group for Aussies who want to play touch rugby. At a pub to which the daily *Métro* suggested Australians go in order to catch the Socceroos games, only two

---

5   The Patriotes were forcefully put down by sword, fire, and brimstone. Some of them were shipped to Sydney and all but one returned to Canada after serving their time. They are commemorated at Canada Bay in Sydney's inner west.

6   Their chalk stand goes: "Notre français n'est pas bon, mais notre café l'est" [Our French isn't good, but our coffee is].

By Joel Mak

On Montréal, Language,
and Being Free

people were dressed in green and gold: myself, and my partner who isn't even Australian. A Griffith man introduced himself after spotting me, but in the course of our expletive-ridden conversation, as we watched Chile take the three points, I learned that he was moving on elsewhere soon. As a holiday destination, the French thing is different, fun, and even exotic for a week or so, but not so much when it is a job — and its attendant benefits such as money, healthcare, and a sense of security — you are after. Language laws mean that the modicum of high school French most people learn in Australia isn't going to help one get by. The 'English-speaking' job is as elusive as the lynx and those who manage to grab one count themselves lucky for they are able to enjoy what Montréal has to offer without having to step into the valley of language darkness.

Therein lies a small paradox: yes, the official language of Québec is French but for the most part, once you've pinned down an income generator, you do not really need to know French to live in Montréal. This is not to say that everyone in Montréal speaks English because this is far from the case. Yet, within a certain radius extending from downtown Montréal, *anglophone* friends can be made at the drop of a "hi", banks and telcos offer a bilingual service, and language jams can easily be navigated with a bit of pointing and nodding. If you can find it within you to start inquiries with *bonjour* you will plant a smile on a *Québécois* face. If you can stand the occasional blunt comment or even rant about you not knowing the local language — which is neither unfathomable nor something exclusive to Québec — then "*c'est correc*".

So, *c'est quoi la problème*? In 2013, Québec's media had a ball
with Pastagate. There was brouhaha and public ridicule for the
Office québécois de la langue française[7] (OQLF) who fined an
Italian restaurant for using Italian words such as *pasta* in their menu
instead of the French equivalent. Dead Obies, a contemporary
Montréal hip-hop collective, has been criticised for using too much
English in their songs. Early in 2014, the then Minister for Language
Diane de Courcy hinted at the prospect of stamping out institution-
alised bilingualism for good. Had her party, the *Parti Québécois*,
won a majority in the April elections they would have — amongst
other initiatives[8] — forced employees in the service industry to drop
the "hi" from the "*bonjour*-hi" customer greeting.

Most recently, 24 business owners in Montréal attempted in vain
to contest fines issued by the OQLF for having used English
in their signage. Salvatore Mascia, from the Court of Québec,
stated that "*La langue française est encore trop fragile pour se
développer sans l'aide du gouvernement québécois*" (The French
language is still too fragile to develop on its own without the aid
of the Québec government). On the defense side, lawyer Brett
Tyler tried to assert the very opposite. Not only is French strong
enough in metropolitan Montréal, forcing constraints on business
owners violates one's freedom of expression.

---

7   The OQLF's mission is to promote the use of French but it often only
generates headlines whenever they fine disobeying enterprises for not conforming to Québec's Charter of the French Language, which includes man-
dating the use of French signage. English and any other language may be
used, but French must have the most prominence, i.e. the font must be bigger
in French.

8   They also forecasted an independence referendum debate (if not a referendum outright) and a Charte des valeurs québécoises, a sort of secularism
charter à la Française which would have banned public sector employees
from wearing religious clothing at work. For this and many other reasons, the
PQ was voted out of power.

On Montréal, Language,
and Being Free

This debate has gone on for decades and it is easy to choose a side and find holes in any argument. For example: if French is indeed too fragile, is signage going to change anything? Or, if French is actually strong enough, then doesn't the use of English symbolise the opposite? What about the geographical context of the debate? These businesses were in downtown Montréal. Rarely do we hear news like this from Rimouski, Chicoutimi, or Saguenay, where French *does* have a stronghold. Montréal with its cultural and economic capital creates its own problem: as English-Canadians and allophone immigrants settle in Montréal, the colour of the city's linguistic façade changes, suggesting a bilingual grey. In this sense, Montréal's bilingualism and cosmopolitanism is not necessarily an accurate reflection of Québec. Arguably however, without the *Québécois* elements of charm, warmth, and an old European *je ne sais quoi*, Montréal is just another North American city — something nobody wishes it to be.

Is Montréal's bilingualism good or bad for Québec? The stand-up comedian Sugar Sammy, known for his bilingual show *You're Gonna Rire*, believes that Montréal's bilingualism is special, something to be not only cherished but supported and brought to the rest of Québec. Yet there's the oft-repeated argument that the use of English or *anglicismes* might degrade the quality of French — rightly considered as the most important feature of Québec. Worse, the number of French speakers might dwindle and taper off in the near future, and along with it the DNA of Nouvelle France.

A man goes to the markets, spots a bunch of spinach that he's been craving for dinner, looks for the price tag and doesn't find it. There are price tags for some of the vegetables, but it is clear organisation isn't the vendor's top priority. So the man clears his throat and in the language of the country, asks the vendor. The vendor, ears perked up like a canine, notices that the man isn't from around town and whether out of spite or bad humour or even unintentionally, makes buying the kilo of spinach difficult for the man, by answering in his own language.

Our man could be from Vancouver on a stroll in Montréal's Jean-Talon Markets. Or, our man could be from China, having just moved from Peking to Guangzhou city. The latter's widespread Cantonese is unintelligible to a Mandarin-speaking Chinese (wo)man from Peking, despite both being branches of the Sino-Tibetan tree. It is a bit of a stretch, but a useful one — Cantonese is as Québec's French is to Canada's English. Proportion-wise, Canada actually has more French speakers than China has Cantonese speakers, even if there are around 60 million Cantonese speakers in Guangdong[9] and more in Hong Kong.

Noticeably, the Chinese government is starting to crack down on China's Cantonese speakers. In August last year, Guangdong TV was rumoured to have received orders to change their broadcasting language. Native speakers of Cantonese found it upsetting and just as they did in 2010, might protest against the central government *en masse*. I'm a Cantonese speaker myself and even though I have never tuned in to Guangdong TV, such reports make me fret and acidic liquids boil around the heart's region. I don't know if language patriotism is acquired or primordial, though I do remember how easy it was to hate schoolteachers who broke up our Cantonese conversations. I felt that language, as a personal piece of identity, should not be something for which one could be punished.

---

9   China has 1.3 billion residents, mostly Mandarin speakers.

On Montréal, Language,
and Being Free

By Joel Mak

Back to Montréal, where I live now and where I perhaps iron-
ically only hear Cantonese in Chinatown. *Linguae francae* are
necessary for political and economic reasons; historically the
nationalisation of regions composed of disparate people was only
successful when linguistic unity was achieved — forcefully or not.
European countries have done that to a degree. China still strug-
gles. The marginalised either hold out against the invaders (to
quote a famous comic) with violence, or happily exist in their co-
coons. Québec has recently exemplified the latter. Having made
French the official language — thus, preempting its possible
extinction — national confidence as a *Québécois* people rose and
separatism (as a political tool to protect oneself from language
loss, amongst other things) has dwindled ever since.

However, legislating language is a thorny issue that creates
imbalances, sometimes at my own expense. The school is not
a personal environment but a nationalised institution in which,
fair game, we should have spoken English. What about Montréal language signage? A business is theoretically not human,
so therefore business owners must adhere to language laws.
What's more, if languages are indeed left on their own terms, I see
a reality show unfurling, where survival of the fittest kicks in[10]. In
the blink of an eye, hundreds of native North American languages,
their protection no longer funded by governments, will disappear.
Will Québec French go? Hard to say. Probably not, but easy to
fear.

All that said, maybe this case was blown out of proportion, as
most language issues can be in Québec (see: Pastagate, above).
The fines received by the said businesses were between $250
and $500. Take it on the chin, some say, and adjust your signs

---

10   Broadcasted in, I assume, the hegemonic lingua franca, laughing as it
provides the commentary.

accordingly. Yet, English signage is not likely to reduce the number of French speakers when most immigrants' children (the most important factor when we talk about language preservation) must learn French. For what it is worth, to live in Montréal without knowing French has its drawbacks. It is to constantly feel like one's missing out on something: public transport emergency notices, the poetry of street chatter, or even one half of the punchlines at Sugar Sammy's show. It is to live on a tight rope, to live outside of one's skin, unable to feel like you belong. Belonging, that other highly personal and subjective concept. Of course, unlike language, one cannot legislate the feeling of belonging.

Who can argue that being monolingual is a good idea? How many times has one heard from a monolingual that (s)he wished (s)he knew another language? All things equal, the acquisition of another language cannot be a bad thing and this is why, without proclaiming to be on the government's or business owners' side, I'm in favour of Montréal.

On top of the dynamic between old and new French, between being North American and European, Montréal captures the constant state of flux of human identity, especially those who were born to or are movers. The code and language – switching one does to feel comfortable mirrors the way we change clothes according to the season. Underneath all the layers of coats, lies a core, housing the deep, vivacious, innate human desire to be free, to be one's own boss. It's no wonder why the passion that accompanies the fervent debates about identity and language runs so high. French or English, Cantonese or Mandarin, Catalan or Castilian Spanish, or bilingualism all round? It is vitally important to use the juridical arena to tease out the wrinkles and iron out the kinks. There's nothing wrong with condemning legislations that award freedom to one group at another's expense,

By Joel Mak

On Montréal, Language,
and Being Free

but it is also necessary to see laws as resulting from societal unease over an issue — whether real or perceived — and that they should be used to guide us as close to harmonious equilibrium as we can get. Let's not forget why there was anxiety and anger in the first place.

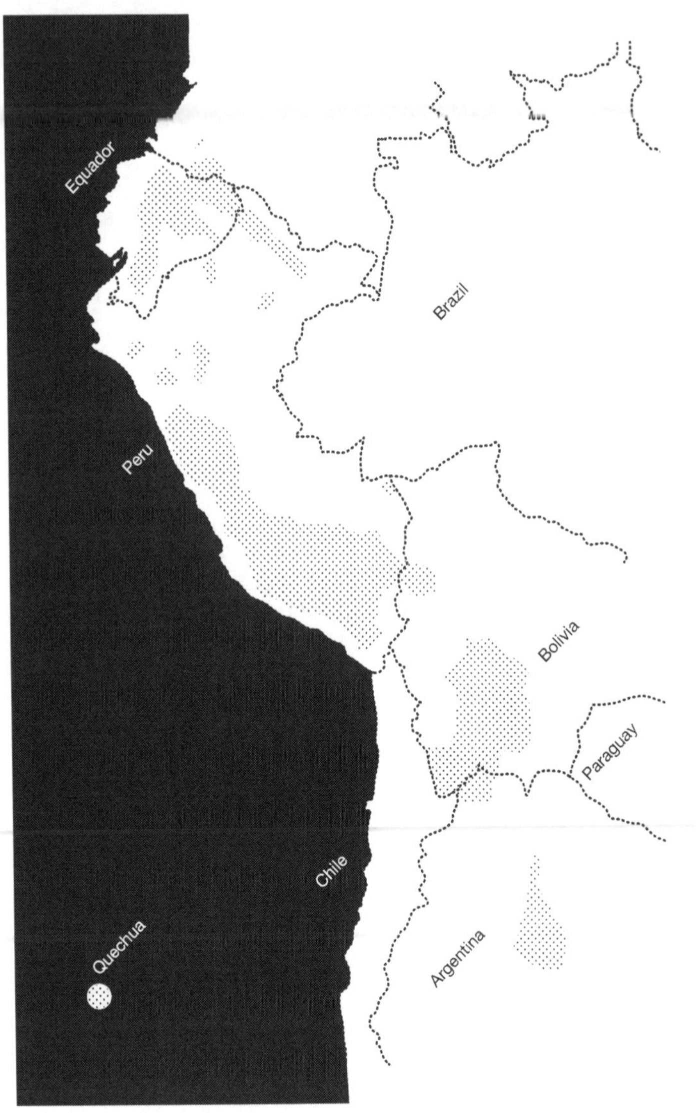

Equador
Peru
Quechua
Chile
Brazil
Bolivia
Paraguay
Argentina

The Quechua Language in the Andean Countries

La lengua quechua en los países de los Andes

By Alex Gentry

Alex Gentry was born in Orange County, California, grew up in Oregon and became passionate about travel and languages from a young age. His endless curiosity for languages led him to fluency in Spanish and Portuguese and additional language skills in Mandarin Chinese, German, Hindi, Russian, Indonesian, and Vietnamese and he plans to continue learning new languages in the future. He has a Bachelor in Anthropology and International Relations from Southern Oregon University. He is an English teacher on italki, a contributor to the nonprofit Wikitongues, and the founder of a language coaching website: The Language Voyager. www.thelanguagevoyager.com.

Since the beginning of my Spanish language studies, apart from my desire to go to Latin America, make Spanish-speaking friends, and learn about Spanish-speaking cultures, my goal was and still is to learn Indigenous languages of Latin America. I am especially interested in the Quechua languages because they are the descendants of the official language of the Inca Empire (Classical Quechua), or as they say in Quechua, "Tawantinsuyu", which means "the four regions/divisions".

My interest in the Quechua language is a story that has lasted a long time, since the year 2008 or 2009 when I initially heard about the language from the Internet. I immediately wanted to learn more about the language. In the bookstore Powell's Books in Portland, Oregon, I found a Lonely Planet phrasebook about Quechua, and without thinking, I decided to buy that little book. In addition, I developed a passion for endangered languages when I saw the 2009 documentary "The Linguists", with linguists Dr. K. David Harrison and Dr. Gregory Anderson of the Living Tongues Institute for Endangered Languages traveling around the world working on many projects to document several endangered languages, including the Chulym language of Siberia, the Chemehuevi language of California and Arizona, the Sora language in Orissa, India, and the Kallawaya language in Bolivia. The last language in this documentary, Kallawaya, is a liturgical language heavily influenced by Bolivian Quechua. However, Bolivian Quechua is the language of daily life in Charazani in the province of Bautista Saavedra while they speak Kallawaya only as the language of their rituals.

I was not able to learn Quechua yet because I was not able to speak Spanish until I began to learn Spanish in 2010. Two years after I started learning Spanish, I intended to learn Quechua on two ocassions: the first time in the year 2012 when I met

By Alex Gentry

The Quechua Language
in the Andean Countries

Desde el inicio de mi aprendizaje del español, aparte de mi anhelo de ir a Latinoamérica, hacer amigos de países hispanohablantes, y aprender sobre sus culturas, mi meta fue y todavía es para aprender las lenguas indígenas de Latinoamérica. Me interesan especialmente las lenguas quechuas, ya que son las descendientes de la lengua oficial del Imperio Incaico (quechua clásico), o como se dice en quechua, "Tawantinsuyu", que significa "las cuatro regiones/divisiones".

Mi interés por el quechua es una historia que ha durado por un largo tiempo, que más menos se remonta al año 2008 o 2009, cuando inicialmente leí sobre esta lengua en Internet. Desde ese momento, quise aprender más sobre este idioma. En la libraría Powell's Books en Portland, Oregon, encontré un libro de frases publicado por Lonely Planet sobre el quechua y sin pensarlo dos veces, compré aquel libro pequeño. Junto a eso cultivé un fuerte interés por las lenguas en peligro de extinción cuando vi el documental "The Linguists" ("Los Lingüistas") en el año 2009, con los lingüistas Dr. K. David Harrison y Dr. Gregory Anderson del Living Tongues Institute for Endangered Languages. Ellos viajaron por el mundo trabajando en muchos proyectos para documentar varias lenguas en peligro de extinción, como la lengua chulym de Siberia, la lengua chemehuevi de California y Arizona, la lengua sora en Orissa, India, y la lengua kallawaya en Bolivia. La última lengua en este documental, kallawaya, es una lengua litúrgica bien influenciada por el quechua boliviano, Sin embargo, el quechua boliviano sigue siendo la lengua de la vida cotidiana en Charazani en la provincia de Bautista Saavedra, por lo que sólo hablan el kallawaya en sus rituales.

Todavía no podía aprender quechua debido a que no pude hablar español hasta que comencé a aprender español en el año 2010. Dos años después, intenté aprender quechua en dos ocasiones:

a Bolivian student that could speak Quechua fluently in addition to Spanish. I tried to meet with him but we only met once as we were both preoccupied with our university studies. I intended to learn it again last year after achieving conversational fluency in Spanish, but instead of focusing on learning Quechua, I pushed Quechua to the side and learned Brazilian Portuguese instead, because I am also very interested in Brazilian culture. And now finally this year I am going to try to learn Quechua to a basic level by the end of the year. During my learning of Quechua I will need the help of Quechua speakers and other students of Quechua, and of course a lot of practice in speaking in order to converse well.

The Quechua languages are spoken in Peru, Ecuador, Bolivia, Chile, Argentina, and Colombia with between 8 to 10 million speakers that covers a huge area of South America, which is quite large for Indigenous languages of the Americas. Generally the situation of Quechua depends on the language policy of every country in which Quechua is spoken. In all these countries, the Quechua language family is a group of endangered languages. In Peru the situation is the worst of all, because the government of Peru, though it has two official languages, only treats Spanish with societal prestige, while Quechua is associated with negative attitudes through the centuries since the time of the conquest. In the conquest era, the Spaniards imposed the institutions of the Catholic Church and the Spanish Crown on the Incas and the other Indigenous peoples and established the Viceroyalty of Peru. During that era, in the Viceroyalty of Peru, Quechua was used as an instrument of evangelization and assimilation of other Indigenous groups to the Quechua language and other widely spoken Indigenous languages like Aymara and Guarani in the same way. During this early period, famous works of Quechua literature like the work Ollantay were composed and also grammars such as Grammar or Art of the Common Language of the Indians of the

By Alex Gentry

The Quechua Language
in the Andean Countries

la primera vez fue en el año 2012 cuando encontré un estudiante de Bolivia que podía hablar quechua con fluidez junto al español. Traté de juntarme con él pero en distintas ocasiones desafortunadamente sólo nos encontramos una vez, ya que estábamos bastante ocupados con nuestros estudios en la universidad. Hice otro intento el año pasado, después de sentirme cómodo conversando en español, pero en vez de enfocarme en aprender quechua, lo dejé de lado y aprendí el portugués de Brasil ya que me interesa mucho la cultura brasileña también. Finalmente, el presente año veré si puedo aprender el quechua, al menos a un nivel básico. Durante mi aprendizaje del quechua necesitaré ayuda de hablantes y otros estudiantes de quechua, y por supuesto mucha práctica para poder conversar bien.

Las lenguas quechuas son habladas en Perú, Ecuador, Bolivia, Chile, Argentina, y Colombia con alrededor de 8 a 10 millones de hablantes, cubriendo una gran parte de Sudamérica, que es bastante grande para las lenguas indígenas de América. Generalmente la situación de quechua depende de las políticas sociolingüísticas de cada país en que el quechua es hablado. En todos estos países, la familia lingüística del quechua está en serio peligro de extinción. En el Perú, la situación llega a ser la peor de todos, porque el gobierno del Perú, a pesar de tener dos idiomas oficiales, coloca al español con mucho prestigio en la sociedad, mientras el quechua es asociado con actitudes negativas desde el tiempo de la Conquista. En la época de la Conquista, los españoles sometieron, a través de instituciones como la Iglesia Católica y la Real Audiencia, a los incas y otros pueblos indígenas, estableciendo el Virreinato del Perú. Durante esa época, en el Virreinato del Perú, el quechua fue un medio de evangelización y asimilación de otros grupos indígenas a la lengua quechua y otras lenguas indígenas con vastas áreas como el aimara y guaraní. Ya en aquellos tiempos, se escribieron obras famosas de la literatura quechua como la obra

Kings of Peru and Lexicon or Vocabulary of the Common Language of Peru. But after the defeat of the rebellion of Tupac Amaru II in 1781 against the Viceroyalty of Peru, Indigenous clothing, customs, and languages were forbidden by the colonial administration in all of the Spanish Empire, not only in the Viceroyalty of Peru. These attitudes, which continued through the independence movements were all led by creoles, descendants of the Spanish colonizers, and as a consequence they imposed their colonial rule on the Indigenous peoples, including the Spanish language. After the independence of the Spanish-American countries from Spain, the official language in all regions of South America was only Spanish (except Brazil, which gained independence from Portugal).

During the following century, a process of linguistic replacement began, or linguistic substitution, of Quechua, Aymara, and other Indigenous languages with the Spanish language, which continues today. However, in the 1950s, speakers of Indigenous languages emigrated to the cities from the country and in the process many lost their languages in favor of replacing them with Spanish. To some extent, this has occurred with the Quechua languages, but much less in comparison with the other Indigenous languages. In school in the colonial era and after the independence of the Andean countries, they developed a shameful attitude in the administrations toward all languages that were not Spanish, and they judged and punished any Indigenous person who tried to speak or use their own language in class. This was done on purpose during the colonial era (especially after the rebellion of Tupac Amaru, because beforehand, the administration of the Viceroyalty of Peru sent missionaries to learn Indigenous languages including Quechua in order to understand the Indigenous people better to convert them and colonize them more easily) and also to convert them to mainstream Spanish-speaking culture.

By Alex Gentry

The Quechua Language
in the Andean Countries

Ollantay, y también se quiso estandarizar la gramática del quechua en libros como Gramática o arte de la lengua general de los indios de los reinos del Perú y Lexicón o vocabulario de la lengua general del Perú. Pero luego de la derrota de la rebelión de Túpac Amaru II en 1781 contra el Virreinato del Perú, la indumentaria, costumbres y lenguas indígenas fueron estrictamente prohibidas por la administración colonial en toda la América española, no sólo en el Virreinato del Perú. Estas políticas, que continuaron entre los movimientos de independencia fueron lideradas por los criollos, descendientes de los colonizadores españoles, y como consecuencia impusieron sus reglas coloniales a los indígenas, inclusive la lengua española. Después de la independencia de los países hispanoamericanos, la lengua oficial en todas regiones de América del Sur (excepto Brasil, que obtuvo su independencia de Portugal) fue solamente el español.

Durante el siglo XIX, comenzó un proceso de reemplazo de lenguas o substitución lingüística, del quechua, aimara, y otras lenguas indígenas por la lengua española que continúa hasta hoy. Sin embargo, en la década del 1950, los hablantes de lenguas indígenas emigraron a las ciudades, provenientes de los campos y en ese proceso, muchos habían perdido sus lenguas, a favor del español. De cierto modo, eso le ha ocurrido a las lenguas quechuas, aunque a menor escala que las otras lenguas indígenas. En las escuelas de la época colonial y después la independencia de los países andinos, existió una actitud de discriminación contra todas lenguas que no eran el español, y así los indígenas eran castigados si eran sorprendidos usando lenguas indígenas en la escuela. Eso fue hecho a propósito, durante la época colonial (especialmente después de la rebelión de Túpac Amaru, porque antes la administración del Virreinato del Perú exigía a los misioneros aprender lenguas indígenas, incluso el quechua, para entender a los indígenas mejor y así convertirlos y colonizarlos) para asimilarlos a la cultura hispana

Essentially in the process they had shamed them to the point that many of the Indigenous people did not want to speak in their own languages, in the same way as policies made in the U.S.A. and Canada against the Indigenous peoples of North America and those made in Australia against the Indigenous peoples of Australia. In an incident demonstrating the atrocities of the colonial administration, the United Syndical Confederation of Peasant Workers of Bolivia said in 1991 that "The school that we knew before made us shut up, it neither permitted us to express ourselves nor to communicate, we feared making mistakes, it punished us morally as well as physically and never treated us with affection or care... In all schools the teacher used to speak in a language that we didn't understand, those who knew some words in Castilian (Spanish) could understand a little something... There were teachers from the country... that didn't use to speak in the classes in their original languages: some because of shame, others because bit by bit they had forgotten."

Over recent centuries, the Indigenous people felt ashamed when they spoke their languages as a result of the persecution, marginalization, and the policy of the colonial and postcolonial governments. In response to the loss of languages, the governments of Peru, Bolivia, and Ecuador formed programs of Bilingual Intercultural Education (BIE) to valorize the languages to the same level in South American societies as Spanish. Generally, the education in Andean countries reflects European cultures, especially Hispanic, instead of multiculturalism and protection. In addition, generally in the process of BIE, the Indigenous peoples were converted from speakers of their native languages to Spanish speakers, essentially a subtractive bilingualism, due to traditional attitudes against the people. BIE generally functions better in practice with foreign languages from outside the Spanish-speaking countries and South America such as English, Portuguese, French, Chinese,

By Alex Gentry

The Quechua Language
in the Andean Countries

dominante. En este proceso, surgió un sentimiento de vergüenza, al punto de que mucha de la gente indígena no quisieron hablar en sus propias lenguas, del mismo modo que sucedió en los E.E.U.U. y Canadá contra los indígenas de América del Norte, o en Australia contra su población aborigen. En una incidente demostrando las atrocidades de la administración colonial, la Confederación Sindical Única de Trabajadores Campesinos de Bolivia dijo en 1991 que «La escuela que hemos conocido antes nos hizo callar, nunca permitió expresarnos ni comunicarnos, teníamos miedo de equivocarnos, nos castigó tanto moral como físicamente y nunca nos trató con afecto y cariño... En todas las escuelas el maestro hablaba en un idioma que no entendíamos, quienes sabían algunas palabras en castellano [español] alguito podían entender... Había profesores de origen campesino... que no hablaban en las clases en sus idiomas originarios: unos por vergüenza, otros porque poco a poco se habían olvidado».

En los siglos recientes, los indígenas sentían vergüenza al hablar sus lenguas, como resultado de la persecución, la marginalización, y la política de los gobiernos coloniales y postcoloniales. En respuesta de la pérdida de los idiomas, los gobiernos del Perú, Bolivia y Ecuador formaron programas de Educación Intercultural Bilingüe (EIB) para valorizar las lenguas al mismo nivel en las sociedades sudamericanas como el español. Generalmente, la educación en países andinos reflejan las culturas europeas, especialmente la hispánica, en vez de fomentar el multiculturalismo y la inclusión de otras culturas o etnias. Junto a esto, generalmente en el proceso de EIB se convierten los indígenas de hablantes de lenguas indígenas en hablantes de español, siendo esencialmente un bilingüismo substractivo, debido a las actitudes tradicionales contra la gente. El EIB generalmente funciona mejor en la práctica con lenguas extranjeras, como el inglés, portugués, francés, chino, árabe, etc. «El plurilingüismo característico de zonas de frontera

Arabic, etc. "Multilingualism characteristic of linguistic border zones can make itself more complex with the addition of one or more foreign languages. So, for example, it happens in Ciudad del Este in Paraguay, where it is frequent that the same individual manages Guarani, Castilian, and Portuguese, languages to which, for reasons of international commerce, they add English in not a few cases, or Korean or any other language of the owners of the establishments settled there".

But in general in BIE, Indigenous languages are treated quite differently from foreign languages, and with the exception of Guarani (the national language of Paraguay and not only spoken by the Indigenous Tupi-Guarani groups), they are still treated as a burden, as an artifact of the past, which is quite similar to the situation of Indigenous languages in North America. This situation is described as "In regard to this characteristic of many Indigenous societies, it is necessary to recognize that, due to colonialism and the adverse conditions that ruled the relations between the Indigenous and non-Indigenous people, mono-lingualism has gradually installed itself as the ideal model of linguistic partition." It seems apparent that this argument in favor of monolingualism exercises a great influence on South America, Central America, and North America through the general pop-ulation. In the case of Quechua languages, one of the Quechua languages of Ecuador, the Kichwa language, is recognized as one of the regional languages and the only official language is Spanish. It is the most spoken language in Ecuador apart from Spanish. Kichwa, or Northern Quechua, currently has 2.5 million speakers in Colombia, Ecuador, and Peru. In Colombia the offi-cial language is also only Spanish and Quechua is only spoken as a small minority language in the extreme south of Colombia. In Bolivia, Argentina, and Chile there are the southern varieties of Quechua, but they are all only predominantly Cusco-Bolivian

The Quechua Language
in the Andean Countries

lingüística puede hacerse más complejo con la adición de uno o más idiomas extranjeros. Así, por ejemplo, ocurre en Ciudad del Este, en el Paraguay, donde es frecuente que un mismo individuo maneje el guaraní, el castellano y el portugués, idiomas a los que, por razones de comercio internacional, se añade en no pocos casos el inglés, el coreano o cualquier otro idioma propio de los dueños de los establecimientos afincados allí».

Pero la situación general del EIB con las lenguas indígenas son diferentes a las de las lenguas extranjeras, y con la excepción del guaraní (la lengua nacional de Paraguay y hablada no solamente por los grupos indígenas de ascendencia tupi-guaraní), siguen siendo vistas como un problema, como un artificio del pasado, siendo semejante a la situación de las lenguas indígenas de América del Norte. Esta situación es descrita esencialmente como «En lo tocante a esta característica de muchas sociedades indígenas, es menester reconocer que, debido al colonialismo y a las condiciones adversas que han regido las relaciones entre indígenas y no indígenas, el monolingüismo se ha instalado gradualmente como modelo ideal de comportamiento lingüístico». Me resulta peculiar que este argumento en favor del monolingüismo ejerza una gran influencia en Sudamérica, Centroamérica, y Norteamérica entre la población general. En el caso de lenguas quechuas, una de las lenguas quechuas en Ecuador, la lengua kichwa, es reconocida como una de las lenguas regionales de Ecuador, pese a que la lengua oficial es español. Sin embargo, es la lengua más hablada aparte del español en Ecuador. El kichwa, o el quechua norteño, tiene en Colombia, Ecuador, y Perú, 2,5 millones de hablantes actualmente. En Colombia la lengua oficial es solamente el español también y el kichwa es solamente hablado como una pequeña lengua minoritaria en el extremo sur de Colombia. En Bolivia, Argentina, y Chile se encuentran las variedades sureñas del quechua, pero el quechua cusco-bolivi-

Quechua in those countries. In Chile there are only thousands of speakers in the extreme north of Chile. It is only one of the minority languages of Chile.

In Argentina also there is a minor presence but in addition to Cusco-Bolivian Quechua there is also the Santiagueño Quechua in the province of Santiago del Estero. In the northernmost provinces of Argentina, Jujuy, Salta, and Tucumán, Cusco-Bolivian Quechua is spoken and the total number of speakers of South Bolivian Quechua in Argentina is around 160,000 speakers and Santiagueño Quechua has around 70,000 speakers. In Bolivia Quechua is an official language along with Aymara, Guarani, and 33 other Indigenous languages in addition to Spanish. Spanish, Quechua, and Aymara are considered the national languages of Bolivia and Bolivia has been the most aggressive proponent of BIE, requiring officials to learn Quechua, Aymara, or Guarani if potential employees want to work in the Bolivian government.

In Peru there is the greatest diversity of Quechua varieties of all the Quechua-speaking countries, but the most common variety is Southern Quechua, which is divided between Ayacucho Quechua and Cusco-Bolivian Quechua, which are mutually intelligible. Ayacucho Quechua is the variety of Quechua closest to the Quechua of the time of the Inca Empire and the Viceroyalty of Peru. Cusco-Bolivian Quechua is the most common variety of Quechua and the one that I want to learn, which also has a large influence from Aymara in the phonology. As mentioned before, the situation of Quechua in Peru is the worst, though Quechua is the official language alongside Spanish. The Quechua people often go to the cities and due to the social prejudice against Quechua, the people forget Quechua out of fear of being judged.

By Alex Gentry

The Quechua Language
in the Andean Countries

ano es predominantemente hablado en esos países. En Chile, solamente hay miles de hablantes en el extremo norte de Chile, siendo una de las lenguas minoritarias en Chile.

En Argentina también hay una presencia menor pero en junto al quechua cusco-boliviano, también está el quechua santiagueño en la provincia de Santiago del Estero. En las provincias más norteñas de Argentina, Jujuy, Salta, y Tucumán, se habla quechua cusco-boliviano y el total de hablantes de quechua sudboliviano en Argentina es cerca de 160.000 hablantes, mientras que el quechua santiagueño tiene cerca 70.000 hablantes. En Bolivia, el quechua es una lengua oficial junto al aimara, guaraní, y otras 33 lenguas indígenas y el español. El español, quechua, y aimara son consideradas las lenguas nacionales de Bolivia y Bolivia ha sido el defensor más insistente del EIB, solicitando a los trabajadores públicos saber quechua, aimara, o guaraní.

En Perú, está la mayor diversidad de variantes de quechua de todos los países quechuaparlantes, pero la variante más común es el quechua sureño, que se divide entre quechua ayacuchano y quechua cusco-boliviano, que son mutuamente inteligibles. El quechua ayacuchano es la variante de quechua más cerca al quechua en el tiempo del Imperio incaico y del Virreinato del Perú. El quechua cusco-boliviano es la variante más común de quechua y es la que quiero aprender, además que tiene una gran influencia del aimara en su fonología. Como dije anteriormente, la situación del quechua en Perú es la peor, pese a que el quechua es una lengua oficial al lado de español. La gente quechua va con mucha frecuencia a las ciudades y debido al prejuicio social contra el quechua, la gente lo olvida por miedo a ser juzgados.

I want to learn Quechua not only because I am interested in the culture, but also because I want to do something for the endangered minority languages in the world. I want to help empower Indigenous communities to use their languages with pride.

References

Luis Enrique López y Wolfgang Küper; (Mayo - Agosto 1999); La educación inter-cultural bilingüe en América Latina: balance y perspectivas. Revista Iberoamericana de Educación - Número 20

By Alex Gentry

The Quechua Language
in the Andean Countries

Quiero aprender quechua no sólo por el hecho que me interesa la cultura, pero también quiero hacer por lo menos algo por las lenguas minoritarias en el mundo, es decir las lenguas en peligro de extinción. Quiero ayudar a alentarlos a utilizar sus lenguas con orgullo.

Referencias

Luis Enrique López y Wolfgang Küper; (Mayo - Agosto 1999); La educación intercultural bilingüe en América Latina: balance y perspectivas. Revista Iberoamericana de Educación - Número 20

La lengua quechua en
los países de los Andes

The Real Meaning
of the 'F' Word

By Lauren Wisgard

Lauren is a fifteen year-old aspiring writer from Adelaide, Australia. Writing her first creative piece at the age of eight, named 'The Starship', she has always been a writer at heart. In 2013 Lauren was shortlisted for the Young Writers Award, and received a certificate of commendation. Coming from a line of writers and journalists, you could say writing is in her blood. Lauren not only writes creative pieces but also loves writing essays, reviews, and persuasive texts. Lauren hopes to write for a magazine when she's older, but would also love to be an author.

Let's talk about feminism.

Oh no, I said the unmentionable 'F' word. Did you cringe at the mention of the word? Did you feel an intangible anger building up inside you? Why is it that this word, which means what everybody truly believes in, equality of the genders, has become a word of aggression, anger, and negativity? Why has the perceived meaning of 'feminism' changed, and when did it happen?

We all acknowledge the bravery of the women of the past, the feminists who went through a living hell so women everywhere could vote and own property. The ones who demanded women have the opportunity of a higher education, who made marital rape a crime, abolished slavery of women, and gave women the right to divorce. The women who let us have access to birth control, the women who made workplace sexual harassment a crime, and enabled us to have a job outside the home.

Yet now, the word 'feminism' or 'feminist' is more often than not used as an insult. Women today reap the rewards that our ancestors fought so hard to get for future generations, but many women don't refer to themselves as a feminist and act like the word is the worst insult in the world.

Googling the word 'feminism' is a recipe for disaster. I expected to find correct information, positive articles, and a community who understands the meaning of the word. To my disappointment I found blogs about why people hate the word, why young women and girls do not define themselves as feminists, and why many find it an insult to be seen as one. The most overwhelming and consistent phrase or opinion on these sites was the constant mutual feeling among these women that they were not

By Lauren Wisgard

The Real Meaning
of the 'F' Word

feminists, because they liked men. One young girl said, "I don't
need feminism because I love men and a women-only world
would be a nightmare."

When I hear the word 'feminism' or 'feminist' my mind immediately conjures thoughts of the brave women involved in the wom-
en's liberation movement in the 1960s and 1970s. But the word
'feminism' was actually around long before that, used in 1837
by a French philosopher named Charles Fourier. He believed in
improving the status of women in society, but he did not advocate
equality of the sexes (ironic, don't you think?).

The first dictionary to give the definition of the word was the Oxford English Dictionary in 1895 reading: "advocacy of the rights of
women (based on the theory of equality of the sexes)."

As the women's liberation movement progressed in the nineteenth
and twentieth centuries, feminism took on the meaning that it is
associated with today: "the theory of political, economic, and
social equality of the sexes."

Like every controversial topic, the meaning of feminism has been
widely and globally misunderstood over time, resulting in the negativity that surrounds it today.

There have been many examples of feminism being regarded in
a negative light and unfortunately, these incorrect definitions have
been spoken publicly by role models and influential leaders of
society, making a significant impact on general society and the
way in which people view the word.

In 1992, Pat Robertson (an American television evangelist and former Baptist minister) said, "The feminist agenda is not about equal rights for women, it is about a socialist, anti-family political movement that encourages women to leave their husbands, kill their children, practice witchcraft, destroy capitalism, and become lesbians."

It is public outbursts like Robertson's that give feminism a negative image, and could be a reason why the term has become so misinterpreted over the years. It could also be the fact that the change in people's views and opinions was a cause of the 'conservative backlash' against liberal issues in the 1970s. The culture of people that rejected or opposed the dominant ideas of liberal issues caused a negative reaction, and because of this, people's views became increasingly fractioned.

Another reason is that people see feminists as "whiny", because some believe we are all equal, and that feminists are complaining needlessly. But we're not.

Let's talk statistics. In Australia, women still earn 80 cents for every dollar a man earns in a lifetime. Now, this 20 cents may not seem like a lot in the scheme of things but it *is* a clear example of the inequality which exists between men and women.

Women make up almost 51 percent of the population, but make up less than 30 percent of elected positions in the federal parliament. Even worse, women hold only *8 percent* of board directorships and 10 percent of executive management positions.[1] These are small battles compared to what women go through

---

1   News.com.au 2014, Women still earning less than men, according to Westpac research, News Limited, accessed 29 January 2015, http://www.news.com.au/finance/work/women-still-earning-less-than-men-according-to-westpac-research/story-fnkgbb3b-1226843742552

By Lauren Wisgard

The Real Meaning
of the 'F' Word

in other countries. In Australia, we have access to education, safety, and rights in the household. In many countries - such as Afghanistan, Iraq, and Sudan – girls don't have equal access to education, something we in Australia take for granted. With young Afghan women for example, only 18 percent of females aged 15 to 24 can read.[2]

Another thing that many people wouldn't have considered is the right to travel. In Australia, women can just hop on a plane and travel to their heart's delight. In Syria, a husband can prevent his wife from leaving the country. In Iraq, Libya, Jordan, Morocco, Oman and Yemen, married women must have their husband's written permission to travel abroad, and they may be prevented from doing so for any reason.

Violence is another major problem, as in many countries around the world there are no laws prohibiting domestic violence against women. In some countries, domestic violence is considered to be a 'private matter' and none of the government's concern.

These are just a handful of examples which describe the reality suffered by millions of women around the world. What we take for granted, they only dream of. Safety, education, health, and overall happiness.

We live in a society that is media orientated. The most seen and viewed people in the media of course are celebrities. Young women look up to and admire these celebrities, and take in everything they say. It saddens me that these influential women

2   U.S Army 2011, Rising literacy in Afghanistan ensures transition, United States, accessed 16 January 2015,
http://www.army.mil/article/59541/Rising_literacy_in_Afghanistan_ensures_
transition/

don't understand the true meaning of feminism, and therefore
are passing that misinformation on to their greatest admirers, the
future generation.

When twenty-two year-old actress Shailene Woodley was asked
in an interview in May 2014 if she was a feminist, she responded
with "No, because I love men, and I think the idea of 'raise women
to power, take the men away from the power' is never going to
work out because you need balance."

Farrah Abraham, a twenty-three year-old American reality show
star, said when asked if she was a feminist during an interview in
2013, "What does that mean - you're a lesbian or something?"
It is clear from comments like these that there is so much misinformation out there, and that even privileged, well-educated
women don't know the correct meaning of 'feminism'. This lack of
clarity is subsequently being passed down to other young wom-
en, giving them an incorrect view on the word.

As part of this younger generation myself, I feel very lucky to
know the real meaning of feminism. I'll admit that last year
I couldn't have told you the meaning. I'm one of few in my age
group to know the real meaning. In Australia, Canada, the US, and
the UK only 30 percent of women consider themselves feminists.
The other 70 percent who don't identify themselves as feminists
do so as they are not familiarised with the true meaning.[3] If they
understood the true meaning, I'm sure that the statistic would
read that 100 percent of women identify as feminists. When
young women were interviewed, the number of self-identifying
feminists only decreased, showing a growing gap in women's understanding of the word for future generations.

---

3   Rufful, D 2015, New Polls Prove That Feminism is DEAD, accessed 15
January 2015,
http://www.youngcons.com/new-polls-prove-feminism-dead/

By Lauren Wisgard

The Real Meaning
of the 'F' Word

When another group of men and women were all interviewed, and asked what they thought it meant to be a feminist, several of them said it is nothing more than hating the male gender. When they found out the real meaning, they said the word should be changed to "humanist" or "genderism".

But if we change the word we lose an important part of history. In time, we will forget those women, the ones whose lives were destroyed so their daughters, granddaughters, and great-granddaughters could have a better life. Who are we to take that away from them?

It is not about "changing" the meaning, as it has always been about gender equality at heart. We simply need to educate people on what it really means. We need to acknowledge the past and learn from it. It is not just women who should be feminists, it is men too. To every male who is reading this: I'm sure that you believe that your mother, wife, sister and daughter all deserve equal rights. Do it for them, and proudly declare yourself a feminist.

Feminism has seen many battles over the years. But the real definition of 'feminist' is: a person who believes in equality of the sexes. Each and every person who identifies as a feminist is an individual.

My name is Lauren, and I am part of Generation Y. I admire and respect the women in my life and the lives of those women who came before me, just as equally as I admire the men in my life. I own red lipstick, and I like dresses. My guilty pleasure is silly rom-coms and I love gossip magazines. I believe in equality of both genders, and I believe that women are just as extraordinary as men, and should be treated accordingly. I am not a stereotypical feminist. I'm not hairy, I'm not manly, and I'm definitely not aggressive, but I am a feminist, and proud to be. Are you?

Kulurdu Marni Ngathaitya!

Sounds Good to Me!

A Kaurna Learner's Guide

Written for Kaurna Warra Pintyanthi

by Rob Amery and Jane Simpson

In Review:
Kulurdu Marni Ngathaitya!
Sounds Good to Me!
A Kaurna Learner's Guide

By Elise López

Elise López was born in the Hills where trees were plentiful and skyscrapers scarce. She now lives in the suburbs with her ever-increasing library of books bursting with the knowledge of a thousand authors. During her spare time she conducts research and writes academic pieces for publication. Her areas of interest include Phraseology, Ethno-linguistics, French literature and film, and Soviet and Post-Soviet discourse. She has studied French, Spanish, German, Russian and Polish, and was taught Morse code when she was little.

"About 150 years since it was last spoken in a day-to-day context… the Kaurna language has come alive again and is used and taught at many places in Kaurna Country."[1]

The Kaurna people are the Indigenous inhabitants of the land surrounding what is now the capital of South Australia, but European settlement in Australia had a devastating effect on the Kaurna language. A process of what the Europeans considered to be rapid civilisation of the Indigenous population caused many of the Indigenous languages to fall dormant. In the case of the Kaurna language, the death of the last native speaker, Ivaritji, meant that the language was no longer spoken after 1929. All that remained of the Kaurna language from that brief period of early colonisation were the documents of two German Lutheran missionaries; Christian Gottlieb Teichelmann and Clamor Wilhelm Schürmann. These two missionaries intended to communicate their work to the Indigenous people using their native tongue. They translated the Ten Commandments and a number of German hymns into Kaurna, but never achieved a full translation of the Bible. Their documents, made up of a sketch grammar, a large number of sentences and a vocabulary of more than 3,000 words, became the manuscript for Kaurna language revival in the late twentieth century. Unfortunately, there are no sound recordings of the language as it was spoken in the nineteenth century and the documents left by Teichelmann and Schürmann have some obvious gaps. Nevertheless, they provided a strong foundation for the revival of the Kaurna language.

By Elise López

---

1   Kaurna Warra Pintyandi. 2015. http://www.adelaide.edu.au/kwp/index/. Accessed 19/3/2015.

In Review: Kulurdu Marni Ngathaitya!
Sounds Good to Me! A Kaurna Learner's Guide

Using his Formulaic Method[2], Rob Amery from the University of Adelaide, with the help of Jane Simpson from the Australian National University, has led the way in the Kaurna language revival movement. Amery's approach, apparent throughout the *Kaurna Learner's Guide*, involves the gradual introduction of small blocks of dialogue, starting with commonly-used exclamations, interrogatives and short responses, which can be introduced into the daily lives of Kaurna language learners. As learners become accustomed to code-switching between Kaurna and English, they can introduce more and more vocabulary and the grammar will become apparent as the learner discovers grammatical patterns. Amery's Method is apparent in the structure of the book, which focuses on words and small phrases well before addressing the issue of grammatical structure.

Unlike most language textbooks, the *Kaurna Learner's Guide* opens with a description of those involved in the Kaurna language revival movement. Complete with photo, bio and comments on each member's perspective of the project, this section shows a strong emphasis on community which is reiterated through much of the book, especially through anecdotes such as the Kaurna name for Professor Mülhausler's ferret (*Marti*, meaning 'bandicoot') and explanations for the reasoning behind why the authors chose particular translations. As the reader works through the book, he or she is drawn in through the perspective of a member of this Kaurna language community. The authors clearly outline how the language is constructed around the sense of community, or 'kinship', therefore providing a contextual basis for the language learner to develop an understanding of how Kaurna language and culture are inextricably linked.

---

2   Amery, Rob. 2004. 'Kaurna Language Reclamation and the Formulaic Method,' presented at the 11th Annual Stabilizing Indigenous Languages Conference at the University of California, Berkeley.

This book is designed to teach people of all levels; from those who have never studied a language (with language learning mnemonics) to more advanced linguists (with a sketch grammar of the Kaurna language). The authors have divided it into two parts. The first is designed to get readers speaking with chapters on specific topics, such as *Tidnaparntu* 'Football' and *Kuya Pirri-wirrkinthi* 'Fishing', and specific contexts, such as *Ngartu-ityangka Wangkanthi* 'Talking with Children' and *Purka-ityangka Wangkanthi* 'Talking with Elders'. The second part looks at more grammatical aspects of language learning, such as writing and forming sentences. Chapter 23, *Kurlana Warrarna Pintyanthi* 'Forming New Words', gives an insight into the process of reviving the Kaurna language.

In the final chapter, language learners will find an array of labelled photos and illustrations. In the same way as a child learns a language by associating what is seen with its label, this chapter indicates the names of body parts, animals, locations and objects, without using English translations. It also uses family photos to illustrate the different terms used by the Kaurna people when referring to their kin. This brings the book full circle to the concept of the Kaurna language and its importance as a community-building tool, which was first indicated by the profiles at the opening of the book.

The *Kaurna Learner's Guide*, along with an upcoming CD and dictionary will provide a comprehensive understanding of the Kaurna language to date. Also, thanks to committees such as Kaurna Warra Pintyandi, which is comprised of Kaurna people, linguists and academics from The University of Adelaide, revivalistic efforts have resulted in Kaurna language courses being made available across the Adelaide region, from preschool to university level. The availability of education is an important step towards seeing Kaurna in action as a functional language.

By Elise López

In Review: Kulurdu Marni Ngathaitya!
Sounds Good to Me! A Kaurna Learner's Guide

Any admirer of linguistic and cultural diversity will take pleasure in the creation of this book. It is a clear and accessible guided tour of the Kaurna language revival movement, designed to reach all audiences. Rather than delving into a theoretical discussion of the authenticity of revived languages, the book takes on a more people-minded approach, looking at the importance of the revival of language as the key to building a sense of community among speakers of a language which was once thought to be lost forever.

Colombia is Not
All About the Lady Snow
and the Big Bootys

Colombia no es solo cocaína y culos grandes

By Laura Rodriguez Castro

Laura is a freelance writer and photographer currently doing her PhD in Sociology. She was born in Colombia and now lives in Queensland, Australia. She likes writing, researching and photographing topics people don't want to talk about. Interested in social issues, gender rights and human rights in general. Passionate about making the world a better place through breaking stereotypes.

Cocaine jokes, sexy dancing requests and the expectation of enormous cleavage are just a few things I have had to cope with for the last five years that I have been away from my own great country of birth, Colombia. Hollywood directors, journalists, celebrities, public figures and the hundreds of people that have heard my ranting in bars and pubs over what Colombia really is, this is for you. The cocaine jokes and the request for sexy dance moves are not something I have enjoyed over the years. You turn my happy evenings into passionate moments of rage. You nurture my feminist views. This article is for you.

First of all, Colombia is not all a tropical island.

The opening scene of the Hollywood movie *Mr. & Mrs. Smith,* starring Angelina Jolie and Brad Pitt, is a humid city at war full of palm trees. It is identified as Bogotá, Colombia. That was my first encounter with the international ignorance surrounding what Colombia is. I grew up in Bogotá for seventeen years and it is definitely cold weather by Colombian standards due to its altitude - 2,640 metres above sea level. Most of the people in Bogotá don't hang out in tropical dresses. Usually we are fully clothed, and for the most part, nights and early mornings are rainy. Sorry to ruin the fantasy.

The movie then goes on to show Brad Pitt and Angelina Jolie smashing tequila shots and having sex in a taxi. Well, here's another fact: tequila is not our drink of choice. Instead, a variety of rums and Aguardiente shots fill our nights out. It is simple: we are not Mexico- and just in case you didn't know, Mexico is in North America.

Most likely our taxi drivers are not open-minded enough to allow you to have sex in our well-known yellow cars, so keep it cool

By Laura Rodriguez Castro

Colombia is Not All About
the Lady Snow and the Big Bootys

Llevo cinco años viviendo en Australia y lejos de Colombia, el país que me vio nacer y crecer. Todos los chistes relacionados con vender, traer o meter cocaína, bailar sexy y esperar que mi escote sea pronunciado han sido algunas de las cosas que he tenido que enfrentar por ser Colombiana en el exterior. Así que este artículo es para los directores de Hollywood, periodistas, celebridades, figuras públicas y todas las personas que han escuchado mis muchos discursos en bares sobre lo que Colombia realmente es. Los chistes relacionados con cocaína y sus expectativas de mi baile 'exótico o sexy' no son algo que haya disfrutado en estos años. Pero gracias, han convertido noches de fiesta en momentos apasionados de ira, resignación y han alimentado aun mas mis posiciones feministas frente al mundo.

Primero que todo, Colombia no es una isla tropical.

La primera escena de la película *Mr & Mrs Smith* con Angelina Jolie y Brad Pitt es una ciudad en guerra, húmeda y llena de palmeras – la ciudad es "Bogotá," Colombia. Este fue mi primer encuentro con la ignorancia internacional que rodea lo que Colombia es. Yo crecí en Bogotá y por los 17 años que viví ahí, es una ciudad que en estándares Colombianos se considera fría, hasta le dicen 'la nevera'. Para los que no saben y quizá para el director de esta película, esto se debe a su altitud – 2,640 metros sobre el nivel del mar. Además, la mayoría de gente en Bogotá no anda vestida en vestido tropicales y normalmente nos vestimos con muchas capas, porque llueve seguido. Lo siento por romper sus fantasías.

Después, la película sigue con Brad Pitt y Angelina Jolie bebiendo tequila y teniendo sexo en un taxi. Bueno, y aquí les va otro dato, el tequila es de México, y así tomemos de vez en cuando, preferimos algo más. Nuestras noches normalmente están acompañadas de ron o aguardiente. Es simple, cada país tiene sus tragos, y por si no sabían, México es en Norte América.

until you get home. But a taxi ride in Colombia is definitely an experience. The best conversations I've had are with these men and women that are much more informed about current issues, geography and sports than a lot of people.

On the subject of getting loose, violence and drugs are not ice-breaker topics to use to meet a Colombian.

I have been fortunate enough to grow up in a safe environment by Colombian standards and war has not affected me directly. But this is obviously not the case for millions of Colombians that have felt the consequences of one of the longest armed conflicts in the world. Countless families, women, kids and whole towns have been devastated for the sake of drugs and power. If this is not enough to make you understand that it is not a joke, patriotism is a pretty big thing in our culture. As passionate as we are with religion and football we feel offended when you joke about our history. If you don't usually joke about war atrocities, don't start here.

Dutch actress and UNICEF ambassador Nicolette Van Dam learned her lesson last year after posting a poorly photoshopped meme of two of our best football players snorting cocaine on Twitter. UNICEF and the Colombian minister for international re-lations asked for her to step down from her UNICEF position and she did so while apologising publicly on Twitter to all Colombians.

Australian radio journalists Matt Tilley and Joe Hildebrand have also joined in with the jokes. On a live podcast they compared Colombians to monkeys and joked about cocaine saying, "I mean everybody has it, is on it, sells it, I hear of people who go there backpacking and say it's crazy. Oh yeah a bit of blow. Everybody has some." They also said stuff like, "Colombians will say, well you know what, we are a bit more than that. We have games and

By Laura Rodriguez Castro

Colombia is Not All About
the Lady Snow and the Big Bootys

Además, nuestros taxistas por amables que sean, no van a tener una mente tan abierta para aceptar que sus pasajeros tengan sexo mientras ellos manejan, así que aguántense las ganas hasta que lleguen a la casa. Eso si, un viaje en taxi en Colombia es una experiencia. Las mejores conversaciones las he tenido con los y las taxistas que muchas veces están mas informados sobre lo que pasa en nuestro país y saben mas de geografía ó deportes que muchas personas.

En el tema de embriagarse, hablar de violencia y el narcotráfico no es la forma de coquetearle a una Colombiana.

He sido una persona afortunada en un país como Colombia y la guerra no me ha afectado directamente. Pero este no es el caso de millones de Colombianos que han sufrido las consecuencias de uno de los conflictos armados mas largos del mundo. Familias, niños y pueblos enteros han sido afectados por el trafico de drogas, la corrupción y el poder. Si esto no es suficiente para que entiendan que esto no es un buen chiste, somos un país bastante patriótico. Así, que como nos apasiona el fútbol y la religión, nos ofende que la gente se ría de nuestra historia. Si no eres de los que normalmente hace chistes sobre la guerra en un bar, no empieces ahora.

La actriz Holandesa y embajadora de UNICEF Nicole Van Dam aprendió su lección el año pasado después de publicar en Twitter una foto de dos de nuestros mejores jugadores de fútbol metiendo cocaína en la cancha. La rama de UNICEF y el Ministro de Relaciones Internacionales hicieron una petición para que renunciará a su cargo. Después de renunciar, ella salió pidiendo disculpas públicamente a todos los Colombianos en Twitter.

En Australia, los presentadores de radio Matt Tilley y Joe Hidelbrand se unieron a los chistes. En una transmisión en vivo compararon a los Colombianos con micos e hicieron chistes sobre la

we kill people too, you know, and coffee. It's not all about drugs."
After a week of this racist podcast there was a petition with more
than 5,000 signatures requesting a public apology for such comments.

It is not only public figures. It has been five years since I left Colombia and the 'lady snow' jokes have been part of my every day
when meeting new people in Australia. There is always that guy
you meet in a bar that is trying to get in your pants and thinks it is
a turn-on to ask if I have smuggled some lady snow from Colombia or if your dad is a drug dealer. It is not funny but it has definitely
been a useful tool to identify douchebags who I wouldn't bang.

To those douchebags: not all Colombian girls are sex symbols
with giant asses, tits and sexy dance moves.

Cleavage, big bootys and fake boobs are how douchebags
picture Colombian women. Like many other Colombian women,
I wasn't born or made with any of these attributes so please stop
being surprised when I say I am from Colombia. As with any
other country, there is such a thing as diversity and that is a great
human trait. Also, I am not a great dancer, my salsa moves are
pretty basic and I hate dancing reggaeton if it means feeling your
crotch rubbing against my leg. So requesting a sexy dance move
when we meet just feeds my feminist rage, rather than making me
giggle and fall right into your arms.

Being sexy is not a quality we are born with. We are individuals
with a personality that is determined by our upbringing. There is
definitely a long way to go for women in Colombia, in terms of
rights and the abolition of male chauvinism, but your international
opinions are definitely feeding into these stereotypes rather than
helping us to move on.

By Laura Rodriguez Castro

**Colombia is Not All About
the Lady Snow and the Big Bootys**

cocaína, "todo el mundo la tiene, la vende, he escuchado historias de mochileros que dicen que es una locura. Si, un poco de perico, todo el mundo lo tiene." También diciendo cosas como, "Los Colombianos dirían bueno somos un poco mas que eso tenemos partidos de futbol y matamos gente y el café – no es solo acerca de las drogas." Después de una semana había una petición con mas de 5,000 firmas para una disculpa pública a esos comentarios.

No son solo figuras públicas. Los chistes sobre la cocaína han sido parte de mi día a día en Australia. Siempre esta ese hombre que conoces en un bar que quiere acostarse contigo y cree que rompe el hielo preguntando si traficas cocaína o si estas relacionada con un narcotraficante. Bueno, pues no es chistoso pero ha sido una buena herramienta de identificar imbéciles con los que nunca me acostaría.

Para esos imbéciles: no todas las Colombianas somos sex symbols con culos grandes que bailan muy bien.

Escotes, culos grandes, tetas de silicona son como los imbéciles se imaginas a las Colombianas. Como muchas mujeres Colombianas, yo no nací, ni quise tener ninguno de esos atributos, así que dejen de sorprenderse cuando digo que soy de Colombia. Como cualquier otro país existe la diversidad y eso es algo increíble de la raza humana. Además, no bailo muy bien, mis pasos de salsa son bien básicos y no me gusta bailar reggaeton si implica sentir la entrepierna de un extraño rozando mi pierna. Entonces, bailar sexy es una opción que todas tenemos, así que la próxima vez que esos imbéciles asuman que todas las Colombianas vamos a bailar sexy, piensen que no todas le comen cuento.

Ser sexy no es una cualidad con la que nacemos y ser individuos con diferentes personalidad es definitivamente una opción al

As with many countries in the world, Colombian culture isn't
perfect, and society has a long way to go in terms of equality
between social classes, gender and race. As a country we still get
more excited about a World Cup game than thousands of cases
of impunity, domestic violence, racism or the national elections,
but that doesn't mean we are resigned to being the butt of the
world's jokes. Especially when they come from people who are
public figures propagating misinformation worldwide.

I will keep going to the usual bar and having the same rants and
conversations with strangers about what Colombia really is.
But just a word of advice… ask before making a sexist, racist or
misinformed judgment about someone's country. It is easier and
I can assure you it will be the better way if you ever want to pick
up a Colombian.

Oh, and by the way it is Colombia not Columbia.

By Laura Rodriguez Castro

Colombia is Not All About
the Lady Snow and the Big Bootys

crecer. Y claro, tenemos un largo camino en términos de reconocer plenamente los derechos de las mujeres y abolir el machismo en Colombia, pero sus opiniones internacionales están contribuyendo a estos estereotipos, en vez de ayudarnos a avanzar.

Como muchos países del mundo, la cultura Colombiana no es perfecta, y tenemos problemas que resolver en términos de equidad de clases, género y raza. Como país aun nos emociona mas el mundial que miles de casos de impunidad, violencia familiar, racismo o las elecciones nacionales. Pero esto no significa que nos hemos resignado a ser motivo de burla en el escenario internacional. Especialmente cuando implica a figuras públicas que por medio de su ignorancia están propagando desinformación.

Entonces, yo seguiré yendo al mismo bar y seguiré dando mis discursos y teniendo conversaciones con extraños acerca de lo que Colombia realmente es. La solución es simple y muchas personas en el exterior ya han optado por aplicarla. Pregunte antes de lanzarse a hacer un chiste sexista, racista o ignorante sobre el país de alguien que acaba de conocer. Es mucho mas fácil, y le aseguro que le va a funcionar mas si se quiere levantar a una Colombiana.

Ah, y por si no sabía, es Colombia no Columbia.

Colombia no es solo
cocaína y culos grandes

THE UNDESIRABLES

'This book may be the only chance Australian citizens have to learn what our government is doing to boat people held on Nauru.'
JULIAN BURNSIDE

INSIDE NAURU

MARK ISAACS

An Interview with Mark Isaacs, Author of *The Undesirables: Inside Nauru*

By Raelke Grimmer

Raelke is a writer and linguist and the Founding Editor of Tongues. She is a PhD candidate in Creative Writing at Flinders University, researching the genre of language journalism and writing a book about monolingualism and multiculturalism in Australia.

Not a day goes by when the issue of "boat people" and Australia's policies in dealing with asylum seekers goes unmentioned in the media. For a long time, the reports which filtered down to the public consisted of fear-mongering and miniscule scraps of information. For too long, asylum seekers have been clumped together as a collective group, dehumanised in the way they are spoken about and stripped of their individual identities. If the public cannot see them as people, the public will not fight for their rights. The media are refused access to Australia's offshore processing centres, and everyone who goes to work in those centres are bound by strict confidentiality agreements. The public is not supposed to know what really goes on in those prisons. We are supposed to be uninformed, and turn a blind eye.

In 2012, the Australian Government made the decision to reopen offshore processing centres for asylum seekers making their way to Australia by boat. Mark Isaacs began working for the Salvation Army in the Nauru detention centre soon after it reopened. Over the time he spent there, he became increasingly frustrated at the way the men locked up in the centre were treated as he witnessed the mental and physical health of the asylum seekers deteriorate. The men on Nauru were locked up without ever knowing if they would be allowed out, isolated from society and the families they'd left behind in search of a safe place to live. Eventually, Isaacs felt he had to speak out about what was really going on in Nauru. His 2014 *The Undesirables: Inside Nauru* reveals the truth of what it is really like on Nauru and the extent of the insufferable conditions those detained there endure. I had the privilege of speaking to Isaacs about his book and his work with asylum seekers.

Isaacs originally became interested in working with asylum seekers while he was undertaking an internship at Oxfam. "This really

By Raelke Grimmer

An Interview with Mark Isaacs,
Author of *The Undesirables: Inside Nauru*

pretty girl told me her mother went to Villawood Detention Centre to visit asylum seekers in Sydney and I said yeah, yeah, I'm heaps interested in asylum seekers, I love asylum seekers," Isaacs says. "I knew that I could then get the mother to say how great I was, it was quite a convoluted plan. Then in going to Villawood Detention Centre, I experienced more or less my first prison, I met my first asylum seekers and heard their stories."

"I was confused as to why, not why we detained asylum seekers, but why we detained them for so long without giving them answers. I couldn't understand why, and this was without knowing any of the policies or histories or anything, just as a real layman going in there and experiencing it firsthand. I couldn't understand why we wouldn't give them their answer, and why we made them wait for years on end, and why we made it so awful. The first asylum seeker I met had rope burns around his neck. Day one, minute one, he said that the Government told him they didn't think he was a real refugee so they were going to send him back to Sri Lanka and so he'd prefer to attempt suicide than go back."

Isaacs was shocked at what he saw in Villawood, and it contradicted everything he knew about Australia. He started to educate himself on what was happening and began to write about it, but, "Even then I was still very naïve and ignorant," Isaacs admits. Roughly six months after Isaacs had visited Villawood, the Gillard Government reopened the offshore processing centre on Nauru. "Soon after the centre reopened, a friend of mine called and told me the Salvation Army were hiring people to go there," Isaacs says. "She told me I should go. At the time I had a pen-pushing job in government and it wasn't anything really adventurous. I'd always had the desire to do work overseas and go to interesting and strange places but I'd never quite figured out how to go about it. This was that opportunity."

Isaacs' friend got the number for him to call off Facebook.
"I called and said, 'I'd like to go to Nauru.' And the person on the
other end of the phone literally said, word for word, 'When can
you go?' And then I was in Nauru."

Isaacs had no experience in social work, had never worked with
asylum seekers and received no training before he left. "There
was no idea on what we would be doing, how we were supposed
to be doing it, who we were supposed to be doing it to, no concept of why we were going there, nothing."

Between October 2012 and June 2013, Isaacs worked on Nauru
for five rotations of between four and six weeks in length. At the
end of each rotation he would return to Australia for a few weeks'
break to recover from the physically and emotionally demanding
conditions he endured on the island. In his book, Isaacs writes
about the men he met in the detention centre and the inhumane
conditions they were subjected to. The book was published in
2014, despite the fact that Isaacs signed a confidentiality agreement stating that he would not speak publicly about what goes
on inside the detention centre, and I ask what made him decide to
speak out.

"It wasn't a one off thing, it was the general degradation of the human spirit in that camp, and not just the men, but the workers there
too. The longer you spend there the worse it gets. You see men
attempting suicide, self-harming, protesting, and you see nothing
getting back to Australia because we aren't allowed to report anything, and the Australian media are not allowed into the camp. The
purpose of the camp is to destroy men's hope, and one of the main
ways of doing that is by isolating them, and there was no way the
Australian public could know, there was no way for the men to get
their story out, and so I guess you know, someone had to do it."

An Interview with Mark Isaacs,
Author of *The Undesirables: Inside Nauru*

By Raelke Grimmer

Isaacs began by writing about what he was experiencing and witnessing. "The first time I started writing was after one of the guys I knew quite well attempted suicide. As time went on more and more things started to frustrate me and I saw more and more things, like abuses of power and human rights, and the angrier I became."

"There were a number of instances that led to the book being published, but it was quite a scary thing to go against my government and break contract and break the confidentiality. But there were small steps of rebellion. It started with the fact of being there as a humanitarian worker, we were there to help the men in a camp that was supposed to deteriorate the men's health. We were already considered a bleeding heart leftie, going against the purpose of the camp, battling against security to gain basic freedoms for the men." Isaacs was then involved in a court case in the camp with lawyer Julian Burnside, who made a case against the Nauruan Government, claiming that the camp was against the Nauruan Constitution. "I wasn't going to get involved," Isaacs says. "Then the head of Wilson Security put in an affidavit which said that the fences were there to protect the men from construction, not to keep them in, and that the recreation program I'd established was an example of the freedoms the men enjoyed. When I saw the work I'd been doing to alleviate the pressure from the men was being used to restrict their freedom even further, I couldn't let that happen. So I spoke in court and then when nothing happened to me there I spoke out publicly, and then when nothing happened to me the book was the next logical step."

I wonder if there have been any negative consequences to Isaacs breaking the confidentiality agreement. "No visible ones, nothing I have experienced," Isaacs tells me. "I'll never be hired by the

Salvation Army again, not that I'm too worried about that. There may be restrictions in government jobs and that sort of thing, but no legal recourse or anything like that."

"It was very cathartic, at the time, to write," Isaacs explains. "The majority of the book I wrote while I was working there, but that was kind of diary-like, I was recounting experiences of what happened and they were usually the most traumatic or funny moments, the emotional moments, so I had the base of the book just from that. When I started to realise I had a good body of work, I started to piece together all those moments, make a narrative, fill the backstory in, why I was there, all those things. Eventually I researched the countries and found out why people were leaving, as back up to what they told me, and interestingly I found a lot of similarities between their stories and the human rights investigation and what was happening. And so then it became not only my experiences, but also an investigation into what was happening. There was a lot of editing out my thoughts on policy, because I didn't want it to be a book on policy. I wanted it to be a book about what happened in the camp. I remember reading the way Primo Levi writes about his experiences in concentration camps and thinking it's the first time I ever really understood what it was like to be in a concentration camp. I wanted to recreate what it feels like to be in a detention centre."

Isaacs certainly achieves this feat. His book is a tantalising read, and it is difficult to come to terms with how the Australian Government could treat human beings so inhumanely. The stories of the men in the detention centre are heartbreaking to read. They are men who have sacrificed everything and left their families behind in the hope of reaching Australia, creating a new life and reuniting with their families in their new country. Instead, they are locked up on a tiny island in the Pacific. In some cases, their families don't

By Raelke Grimmer

An Interview with Mark Isaacs,
Author of *The Undesirables: Inside Nauru*

believe they are locked up. Instead, they believe the men are free in Australia and simply do not wish to share the wealth with them. Wives remarry, find other lives. All the while, the men are locked up in insufferable conditions with no knowledge of how long they will remain there for.

"Of the over 500 men I worked with, not one has received a refugee determination status yet. That's been 29 months now since they arrived in Nauru, let alone their time on Christmas Island," Isaacs says. "The month after I left the island there was a fire that burnt down the camp and of the 500 men, 153 were arrested and charged with arson, riot and unlawful assembly. The others were given a choice. They could sign a document to stop their processing and be sent to Australia to restart their processing, or they could stay on Nauru and never be resettled in Australia. So obviously they all chose the former. They all got transferred to detention centres in Australia, and the majority were out February last year. So in that sense they've all been waiting about 17 months because they had to restart their processing. All of those guys are on bridging visas, waiting in the community, and they're all just starting to get work rights. A year after being released."

"There were 153 men charged. Many stayed in Nauru for over a year. Of these, some were transferred to the Darwin detention centre and remain there. Worse still, there are a small number who are still in Nauru. Of the 153 men only 2 were convicted, and both of them had their convictions overturned on appeal."

Listening to Isaacs speak, it is difficult not to feel ashamed as an Australian for what our government is doing to asylum seekers. "I did go through a period of thinking well, you know, what the fuck? And also an incredible shame. But at the same time, this isn't like a one-off, we went from zero to detention centres.

It's been this slow rotting of public opinion and so, for me, it's an example of showing how if you let things fester and don't stand up and have someone fighting back then this is what happens," Isaacs says. "If you continually say people are illegal, then it makes sense to put them in a prison. So I think there are a few people who can be considered responsible for manipulating widespread public opinion and they should feel ashamed for what they are doing. I think for the majority of Australians they're ignorant to what is happening and it is difficult to know everything. And so I'm not ashamed of all of Australia, but I am definitely disappointed in the way we are going."

Isaacs now works as an asylum seeker case worker at Settlement Services International, working specifically with asylum seekers who have been granted bridging visas. "When they are first released from detention, and the policies have changed so much in the past year and a half, but essentially they are given six weeks accommodation funded by the government, and they are expected to find alternative forms of accommodation within that time. For the majority of the time I have worked they do not have work rights, they do not have the same supports as refugees, they more or less have no supports. They receive approximately $450 a fortnight, and they have the option for rent assistance, and with that they're expected to pay rent, to pay transport, to pay food, etc, it's a very bleak lifestyle and there is nothing to do. It didn't take long for us to start to see very similar symptoms to what we saw on Nauru, just over extended periods of time and on a less intense scale, but we have seen guys fail miserably and many guys see trauma counsellors."

Isaacs explains that the government has started to introduce work rights, but those rights come at a cost. "They get work rights, but they can't ever get permanent protection in Australia. They can

By Raelke Grimmer

An Interview with Mark Isaacs,
Author of *The Undesirables: Inside Nauru*

only ever have temporary protection. Either a three year or a five year visa, and even if they are assessed to be a refugee, they are reassessed every three or five years, saying, can you return to your country? They never have a sense of stability. On top of that, they can't reunite with their families, they will never be allowed to bring their families over, even though they have been found to be refugees. It is part of the same deterrence policy. You're trying to create as few incentives as possible to come to Australia. The guys who are in Australia now are lucky to be here, because anyone who comes to Australia by boat now is supposed to be resettled in either Nauru, or Cambodia."

It is hard to accept that there is not a humane alternative to current government policies, in particular because Australia's stark policies on asylum seekers are starting to get attention around the world. At the time of writing, Australia's treatment towards asylum seekers was found to be in breach of the UN's Human Rights Convention and the International Convention Against Torture.

"We need a proper discussion amongst our leaders that discusses the truths of the situation," Isaacs says. "In the anti-boat people segment there are legitimate concerns about trying to control the numbers, but the way we've gone about it is so far from the reality of the situation and the only way you can really see it is if you demonise them and I don't understand why people continue to talk in mistruths and lies. We can have very similar policies that restrict people from coming to Australia by boat, but just offer humane alternatives. That's the first thing. Let Australians understand and know what the real issues are here. There's no discussion happening in the national media. The left-wing are not looking at the situation realistically either, saying, 'let them all come in!' that's not the answer either, we need a proper discussion."

For the asylum seekers who are granted refugee status and the right to live in Australia, there is work to be done, too. "We need to have more support," Isaacs says. "I think work rights is an amazing start, but we need better orientation into Australia, and to foster a sense of trust and welcoming and not make them feel like second-class citizens and not treat them like second-class citizens."

I ask Isaacs if he thinks it is beneficial for young people who wish to work with asylum seekers to spend time working or volunteering at a detention centre. "I think it can be worthwhile, but I don't think it's necessary. I personally have my own views, and I don't think that anyone should ever have to follow me, but for me, if I'm talking about something then I want to experience it," Isaacs says. "But they're horrible places. I don't have to work in Villawood to know it is a horrible place. But I have more authority because I have gone and done those things. There are more and more accounts coming out, so people don't have to go to Nauru to know Nauru is awful, they can read things like my book, or the Serco comic[1]. Those things are out there, there are definitely ways to research it. My encouragement would be to go and meet the asylum seekers, meet refugees, try and get as many different views as possible, because some are very against people smugglers and don't want any more people coming by boat, and some aren't. It is extremely complicated, but the best way to research this is to meet the people who have made the journey."

The Undesirables: Inside Nauru is a great place to start for anyone who wishes to learn more about the stories of the people who come by boat to Australia seeking asylum. Organisations such as the Asylum Seeker Resource Centre (ASRC) provide aid, advoca-

---

1   An online comic "At Work Inside Our Detention Centres: A Guard's Story", http://serco-story.theglobalmail.org/

By Raelke Grimmer

An Interview with Mark Isaacs,
Author of *The Undesirables: Inside Nauru*

cy and health services for asylum seekers and are always looking for donations and volunteers for the many services they provide. It is people like Isaacs and places like the ASRC that enable us to see the truth. And once we know the truth, we can create change.

Mia san Mia:

The Unique Bavarian Language and Culture

Die einzigartige bayrische Sprache und Kultur

Da oanzigartige boarische Dialekt und sei Kultur

By Ramona Fellermeier

Ramona Fellermeier is a German life coach, travel blogger and writer. She has a passion for travelling, languages and aviation, as well as sports and healthy living. Ramona has been travelling the world for the past two years and shares her work and stories on both her travel blog Always Happy Travels and her website www.ramonafellermeier.com.

Dirndl, Lederhosn and Bier – most German clichés are not really as German as many foreign visitors think. That is because many of these clichés actually originate in Bavaria, one of Germany's 16 states. Bavaria lies in the idyllic Alps in southern Germany, and is also a term for many non-Germans (not just in football!) and is known for its very unique, noteworthy and amiable mentality. In Bavaria the clocks (just like the language) still run differently.

I am a born and bred Bavarian, born in Altötting, a place of pilgrimage in the vicinity of ex-Pope Benedict XVI's home and raised in a small town not far from Munich. My family is 100% Bavarian and therefore from birth I was brought up speaking the Bavarian language. The Bavarian way of life is in my blood and I am very proud of that heritage. But why is Bavaria now so different from the rest of Germany? I can put it best by describing a few Bavarian sayings, as for every culture language is one of the main identifying features.

We best begin with this very famous saying: Mia san mia. If you're speaking with a Bavarian about their home and this sentence is mentioned, then you know: this person knows where they come from. And where their heart lies. And what they are proud of. Namely, their homeland.

The saying Mia san mia (in German, Wir sind wir, and in English, we are who we are) has many applications, but only one meaning. It is mentioned when Bavaria is compared to the rest of the world, in especially sentimental moments, and mostly associated with football. Germany's most successful and world famous football club, FC Bayern München, has made the saying their motto and slogan. Mia san mia- no one can defeat us. Mia san mia- full of confidence.

By Ramona Fellermeier

Mia san Mia:
The Unique Bavarian Language and Culture

This healthy, but usually very strong, self-confidence has become something of a Bavarian trademark over time. And a lack of trademarks is certainly not an issue here in Bavaria. Most of you will have heard of the legendary Oktoberfest (or even have experienced the two-week madness of the event) and King Ludwig's magnificent castles, such as Neuschwanstein or Herrenchiemsee are well-known to many. Everyone has an image of our unique and somewhat strange costume- Drindl for the women and Lederhosn for the men- in their heads and Bavarian beer is also famous well beyond the state borders. But what about the Bavarian language?

Essentially, Bavarian is merely a dialect, but a look at history makes it clear why the rest of Germany has such a problem with the Bavarian language. Historically, Bavarians had many more close relations with Austria than with the northern part of Germany (then called Prussia). Bavaria was distanced from Prussia, while the Austrian-Hungarian Empire was a lively exchange. This also had an impact on dialect and language. Today, Bavarians and Austrians can understand each other without problems, in particular when both parties speak dialects. A northern German, however, has a big question mark on their face, when they hear Bavarian for the first time. Same country, completely different manner of understanding!

The Bavarian language is rich with picturesque expressions and unique words. One of my favourite words is *fei*. *Fei* cannot easily be translated into German or English and really has no specific meaning. With *fei* as a filler word, a Bavarian can refine every sentence. For example:

Mei, heid is fei wieda koid. Ja do muss i fei glei meine Handschuah eipacka, sonst friads mi wieda wia'd Sau. Und dass'd ma

*fei ja ned vagisst, de Fensta dahoam zua zum macha. Do hamma
fei letzt's Jahr an bessan Winta ghabt!*

And in English:

*It is so cold today! Therefore I better pack my gloves, otherwise I'll
freeze. And I better not forget to close the windows at home. Last
winter was really so much better!*

In reality, the word is not used in every sentence, but according
to Bavarian grammar (which doesn't really exist), it is theoretically possible. And the best thing: only a Bavarian knows where
to use *fei* in a sentence. There are no rules, and in the end it is
a gut feeling. And that goes for the entire Bavarian language: no
definite rules, no fixed spelling and countless regional differences
in grammar, vocabulary and pronunciation.

And because it is so beautiful, here are three more examples from
the Bavarian language:

1   The Double Negative

Example: I hob jetz koa Zeit ned. (I have no time)

One of the most widely used features in the Bavarian language
is the double negative. Theoretically, a statement with a double
negative actually makes a positive statement- not so in Bavarian.
In most cases, it consists of a form of *koa* (no) and the word *ned*
(not) and can be applied in all possible everyday situations. By
using this linguistic feature, the recipient of the information has no
doubt that the person really has no time.

2   Strong Expressions

In addition, Bavarian is full of strong and colloquial expressions: it is really easy for a person to say what they think. And then once something comes across strong - *ja mei*. As for cursing in Bavarian the rules are orderly:

- Zefix! (From the Bavarian word Kruzifix, a Jesus figurine nailed to the cross, with a religious, Catholic meaning.)
- Ja leck mi am Oarsch! (Kiss my ass. A very strong expression for surprise.)
- Du Zipfeklatscher! (Idiot!)

We Bavarians are in principal very peaceful folk and when we complain, it is mostly about the weather, football or local politics. In Bavarian *Granteln* means to rant or to complain and it is part of our mentality. And while we can get very annoyed at times, it doesn't really last long. And most of the strong expressions are usually less severe than intended.

3   The Bavarian Conjunctive

We Bavarians have such beautiful swear words and curses, but we can also be polite! So in linguistic terms ensures the Bavarian conjunctive. Some use and understand it, others don't use it but understand it nonetheless. Non-Bavarians don't use it, and also don't understand it. What is the Bavarian conjunctive? It is best to explain with some examples:

- Dadn sie mir den Stui frei hoitn?
  (Could you please save the chair for me?)
- I waar jetzad do. (I'm there now.)
- Da Kaffää warad fiate! (The coffee is cold!)

The Bavarian conjunctive contains not only obvious information, but also another, subliminal meaning. In the third example, let yourself not only deduce that the breakfast coffee is ready, but also that the woman of the house is presumably already annoyed and is sitting at the kitchen table waiting until the rest of the family eventually arrives very casually. Most can only understand this fine nuance with an experienced ear and correct interpretation.

By which we come to an important fact: Bavarian is easy to speak if it is a person's mother tongue. Due to a lack of rules and spelling which is not definitive, there is no limit to an individual's interpretation of most Bavarian words, and that is the greatest difficulty for beginners. It is best if a person can learn Bavarian- the culture as well as the language- by spending time in the region. The possibilities are then endless, as Bavaria not only has countless customs and traditions to offer, but also a multitude of attractions and breathtaking nature, especially in the Alps. Those who are interested in learning a few Bavarian words (or who had to look up a few words from this article), should take a look at the vocabulary list below.

Servus and merce!

By Ramona Fellermeier

Mia san Mia:
The Unique Bavarian Language and Culture

Bavarian Vocabulary

Bayrisch	Deutsch	Englisch
(die) Brezn	(die) Breze	Pretzel
(der) Bleschl	(die) Zunge	Tongue
Dahoam	Zuhause	At home
(das) Dirndl	(das) Mädchen /oder Name für Traditionelles Kleid	Girl /or name for traditional dress
(der) Fuaßboi	(der) Fußball	Soccer
Helf da God!	Gesundheit!	Bless you!
Iwo!	Stimmt nicht!	That's not right!
(die) Maß*	1l Bier	1l beer
Merce	Danke	Thank you
Mia	Wir	We
Minga	München	Munich
(der) Oachkatzlschwoaf	(der) Eichhörnchenschwanz	Tail of a squirrel
Prost*	Prost	Cheers
Schiach	Hässlich	Ugly
Servus	Hallo; Tschüss	Hello; Bye
Spotzal	Schatz; Liebling	Darling; Liebling
Wepsad	Aufgedreht; unruhig	Hyper
Zuagroaster	Fremder	Foreigner
Zünftig	Ausgelassen; Heiter	Jolly

* A very important word for the Oktoberfest

Dirndl, Lederhose und Bier – die meisten deutschen Klischees
sind eigentlich gar nicht so deutsch wie viele Besucher aus dem
Ausland denken. Und das liegt daran, dass viele dieser Klischees
ihren Ursprung in Bayern haben.

Bayern, eines der 16 deutschen Bundesländer und ganz idyllisch
im Süden Deutschlands am Rande der Alpen gelegen, ist auch für
viele Nicht-Deutsche ein Begriff (und das nicht nur im Fußball!),
und der Freistaat besitzt eine ganz eigene und bemerkenswert
liebenswürdige Mentalität. In Bayern gehen die Uhren (genau wie
die Sprache) auch heute noch anders – wie und warum werde ich
euch in diesem Artikel etwas näher bringen.

Als waschechte Bayerin wurde ich im Wallfahrtsort Altötting
geboren (dort ganz in der Nähe ist übrigens auch Ex-Papst Benedikt XVI zu Hause) und bin in einer Kleinstadt in der Nähe von
München aufgewachsen. Meine Familie ist zu 100% bayrisch und
somit bin ich auch sprachlich schon von Geburt an mit dem bayrischen Dialekt aufgewachsen. Die bayrische Lebensweise steckt
mir praktisch im Blut, und darüber bin ich sehr stolz. Und warum
ist Bayern jetzt so anders als der Rest Deutschlands? Lasst es
mich am besten mit ein paar bayrischen Ausdrücken beschreiben,
denn Sprache ist für jede Kultur eine der Hauptidentifikations-
merkmale*.

Fangen wir doch am besten mit diesem sehr beliebten Ausdruck
an: Mia san mia. Wenn dir ein Bayer von seiner Heimat erzählt
und diesen Satz erwähnt, dann weißt du: Dieser Mensch weiß wo
er herkommt. Und woran sein Herz hängt. Und worauf er stolz ist.
Nämlich auf seine Heimat.

By Ramona Fellermeier

Mia san Mia:
Die einzigartige bayrische Sprache und Kultur

Dirndl, Lederhosn und Bier – de meistn deitschn Klischees san eigentlich gar ned so deitsch wia vui Bsuacha ausm Ausland dengan. Und des liegt do dro, dass vui vo dene Klischees ihran Uasprung in Bayern ham.

Bayern, oans vo de 16 deitschn Bundesländer und ganz idyllisch im Südn von Deitschland am Rand vo de Alpen glegn, is a fia vui Breissn a Begriff (und des ned nua im Fuaßboi!), und da Freistod hod a ganz eigene und bemerkenswert liabensweate Mentalität. In Bayern gengan de Uhren (genauso wia'd Sprach) a heid no anders – wia und warum werd i eich in dem Artikel a bisserl näher bringa.

Ois waschechte Bayerin bin i im Wallfahrtsort Altötting geborn worn (do in da Nähe is fei a da Ex-Papst Benedikt XVI dahoam) und aufgwachsn bin i in am Kaff glei neba Minga. Mei Familie is zu 100% boarisch und desweng bin i a sprachlich scho von Gebuart o mim boarischen Dialekt aufgwachsn. De boarische Lebensweise steckt ma quasi im Bluad und do bin i recht stoiz drüba. Warum is Bayern denn jetzad a so anders ois des übrige Deitschland? Am besten lossts mi des mid a paar boarische Gsatzl erklärn, weil de Sprach für a jede Kultur des oiawichtigste is.

Fang ma doch am besten glei moi mid am recht beliebtn Gsatzl o: Mia san mia. Wenn da a Bayer vo seina Hoamad vazoid und genau den Satz erwähnt, dann woast: Der woas wo a herkimmt. Und wo sei Herz hängt. Und worauf a stoiz is. Nämlich auf sei Hoamad.

Des Gsatzl Mia san mia hod zwar vui Owendungen, aber nua oa Bedeitung. Es weard gsogt, wenn se Bayern mim Rest vo da Woid vagleicht, in bsunders sentimentale Momente und mid Abstand am meistn im Fuaßboi. Deitschlands erfoigreichster und auf da ganzn Woid bekannter Fuaßboiverein FC Bayern Minga hod si

Der Ausdruck Mia san mia (auf Deutsch Wir sind wir) hat viele
Anwendungen, aber nur eine Bedeutung. Er wird erwähnt, wenn
sich Bayern mit dem Rest der Welt vergleicht, in besonders sen-
timentalen Momenten und mit Abstand am meisten im Fußball.
Deutschlands erfolgreichster und weltweit bekannter Fußballv-
erein FC Bayern München hat sich den Ausdruck zum Motto und
Slogan gemacht. Mia san mia – uns kann niemand besiegen. Mia
san mia – und strotzen nur so von Selbstbewusstsein.

Dieses gesunde, jedoch meist sehr stark ausgeprägte Selbstbewusstsein ist im Laufe der Zeit so etwas wie ein bayrisches
Markenzeichen geworden. Und an Markenzeichen mangelt es
uns hier in Bayern tatsächlich nicht: Die meisten von euch haben
bestimmt schon einmal vom legendären Oktoberfest gehört
(oder sich gar selbst in den gut zweiwöchigen Wiesn-Wahnsinn
gestürzt) und auch König Ludwigs Prachtbauten wie beispielsweise Neuschwanstein oder Herrenchiemsee sind Vielen ein Begriff.
Man hat ein Bild unserer einzigartigen und etwas seltsamen
Tracht – Dirndl für die Frau und Lederhose für den Mann – im Kopf
und auch das bayrische Bier ist weit über die Ländergrenzen hin-
weg bekannt. Aber wie sieht es mit der bayrischen Sprache aus?

Im Grunde genommen ist Bayrisch lediglich ein Dialekt, aber
ein Blick in die Geschichte macht deutlich, warum der Rest
Deutschlands so einige Probleme mit dem Bayrischen hat:
Historisch gesehen hatte Bayern schon früh viele engere Beziehungen mit Österreich als dem nördlichen Teil Deutschlands
(damals das sogenannte Preußen). Von Preußen distanzierte man
sich, während mit dem Königreich Österreich-Ungarn ein reger
Austausch bestand. Das hatte auch einen Einfluss auf Dialekt
und Sprache. Heutzutage verstehen sich Österreicher und Bayern
ohne Probleme (auch und vor allem wenn beide Parteien Dialekt
sprechen). Ein Norddeutscher jedoch hat ein großes Fragzeichen

By Ramona Fellermeier

Mia san Mia:
Die einzigartige bayrische Sprache und Kultur

des Gsatzl zum Motto und Slogan gmacht. Mia san mia – uns konn koana schlogn. Mia san Mia – und strotzn nur a so vor Selbstbewusstsein.

So a gsunds, aba meist recht stark ausprägts Selbstbewusstsein is im Laufe da Zeit so wos wia a boarisches Markenzeichn woan. Und an Markenzeichnen hamma in Bayern tatsächlich ned z'wenig: De meistn vo eich ham bestimmt scho moi vo da legendären Wiesn ghead (oder sie sogar soiba in den guad zwoa Wocha langan Wahnsinn gstürzt) und a de Prachtbauten vom Kine wia Neuschwanstein oda Herrenchiemsee san vui Leid a Begriff. Man hod a Buidl vo unsana oanzigartigen und a bisserl soitsama Tracht im Kopf – Dirndl für'd Frau und a Lederhosn für'n Mo – und a as boarische Bier is weit bis üba de Landesgrenzn weg bekannt. Aba wia schauts nachad mim Boarischen aus?

Boarisch is eigentlich a Dialekt, aba a Blick in die Gschichte macht deidlich warum da Rest vo Deitschland so einige Probleme mim Boarischen hod: Historisch gseng hod Bayern scho fria vui engere Beziehungen mid Österreich ghobt ois mim nördlichen Teil vo Deitschland (damois des sogenannte Breissn). Von de Breissn hod ma se distanziert, während mim Königreich Österreich-Ungarn a reger Austausch bstanden hod. Des hod a an Einfluss aufn Dialekt und d'Sprach ghabt. Heid vastengan se d'Österreicher und Bayern ohne Probleme (a und vor allem wenn beide Parteien Dialekt sprechan). A Breiss hod jedoch a groaß Fragezeichen im Gsicht, wenn a zum ersten Moi Boarisch heart. Gleichs Land, komplett unterschiedliche Verständigungsweise!

As Boarische is reich an buidhaften Wendungen und oanzigartige Wörta. Oans vo meine Lieblingswörta is fei. Fei konn weder ins Deitsche no ins Englische übersetzn wearn und hod eigentlich im Gesicht, wenn er zum ersten Mal Bayrisch hört. Gleiches Land, komplett unterschiedliche Verständigungsweise!

Das Bayrische ist reich an bildhaften Wendungen und einzigartigen Wörtern. Eines meiner Lieblingsworte ist fei. Fei kann weder ins Deutsche noch ins Englische übersetzt werden und hat eigentlich keine eigene Bedeutung. Mit fei als sprachlichem Lückenfüller kann ein Bayer so gut wie jeden Satz verfeinern. Ein Beispiel:

Mei, heid is fei wieda koid. Ja do muss i fei glei meine Handschuah eipacka, sonst friads mi wieda wia'd Sau. Und dass'd ma fei ja ned vagisst, de Fensta dahoam zua zum macha. Do hamma fei letzt's Jahr an bessan Winta ghabt!
Und jetzt auf Deutsch:

Heute ist es aber wieder kalt. Da muss ich doch gleich meine Handschuhe einpacken, sonst friert mich wieder so. Und vergiss ja nicht, die Fenster zu Hause zu schließen. Da war der letzte Winter aber wirklich besser!

In der Realität wird das Wort natürlich nicht in jedem Satz benutzt, aber gemäß der (eigentlich nicht existierenden) bayrischen Grammatik ist es theoretisch möglich. Und das Beste: Nur ein Bayer weiß, wo im Satz er fei zu benutzen hat. Es gibt keine Regeln, und am Ende entscheidet das Bauchgefühl. Und das gilt für die komplette bayrische Sprache: Keine definierten Regeln, keine festgelegte Schreibweise und unzählige regionale Unterschiede in Grammatik, Wortschatz und Aussprache.

Und weil es so schön ist gibt es jetzt noch drei weitere Besonderheiten aus der bayrischen Sprache:

Mia san Mia:
Die einzigartige bayrische Sprache und Kultur

koa eigene Bedeutung. Mid fei ois sprachlichem Lückenfüller ko
a Bayer so guad wia jedn Satz verfeinern. A Beispui:

Mei, heid is fei wieda koid. Ja do muss i fei glei meine Handschuah
eipacka, sonst friads mi wieda wia'd Sau. Und dass'd ma fei ja
ned vagisst, de Fensta dahoam zua zum macha. Do hamma fei
letzt's Jahr an bessan Winta ghabt!

In da Realität weard as Wort natürlich ned in jedem Satz braucht,
aba gemäß da (eigentlich ned existierenden) boarischen Grammatik is es theoretisch möglich. Und as Beste: Nur a Bayer woas, wo
im Satz er fei hernemma ko. Es gibt koane Regeln, und am End
entscheidt as Bauchgfui. Und des guid für'd komplette boarische
Sprach': Koane definierte Regeln, koa festglegte Schreibweise
und unzählige Unterschiede in Grammatik, Wortschatz und Aus-
sprach.

Und weil's so sche is gibt's jetzt no drei weitere Bsunderheitn ausm
Boarischen:

1 Die doppelte Verneinung

Beispiel: I hob jetz koa Zeit ned. (dt.: Ich habe jetzt keine Zeit)
Eine der am weitesten verbreiteten Besonderheiten der bayrischen Sprache ist die doppelte Verneinung. Theoretisch wird
eine Aussage bei doppelter Verneinung wieder positiv – nicht so
im Bayrischen. Meistens besteht sie aus einer Form von „koa"
(keine) und dem Wort „ned" (nicht) und kann in allen möglichen
Alltagssituationen angewendet werden. Bei Verwendung dieser
sprachlichen Besonderheit lässt man dem Gegenüber keinen
Zweifel, dass man jetzt wirklich keine Zeit hat.

2 Derbe Ausdrücke

Das Bayrische strotzt außerdem nur so von derben und umgangssprachlichen Ausdrücken: Es wird ganz einfach gesagt, was
man denkt. Und wenn das dann doch einmal etwas derber rüber
kommt – ja mei. Und geflucht wird in Bayern in der Regel ordentlich:

- Zefix! (Vom bayrischen Wort Kruzifix, eine ans Kreuz
  genagelte Jesusfigur und somit mit religiöser, katholischer
  Bedeutung)
- Ja leck mi am Oarsch! (Leck mich am Arsch! Sehr derber
  Ausdruck der Überraschung)
- Du Zipfeklatscher! (Blödmann! Idiot!)

Wir Bayern sind grundsätzlich ein äußerst friedvolles Völkchen
und wenn wir uns beschweren, dann meist über das Wetter, den
Fußball oder die lokale Politik. Granteln bedeutet im Bayrischen
„schimpfen" oder „sich beschweren" und ist Teil unserer Mentalität. Wir können zwar auch einmal richtig sauer werden, aber
das hält meist nie wirklich lange an. Und die meisten derben
Ausdrücke sind meist weit weniger schlimm als gemeint.

1   Beispui: I hob jetz koa Zeit ned.

Oans vo de am weidesten verbreitesten Bsunderheitn vo da boarischen Sprach' is de doppelte Verneinung. Theoretisch weard a Satz
bei da doppelten Verneinung wieda positiv – ned so im Boarischen.
Meistens bstäds aus ana Form vo „koa" und „ned", und ko in olle
Alltagssituationen hergnumma wearn. Bei da Verwendung vo dera
Bsunderheid losst ma seim Gegenüber koa Zweife, dass ma jetzad
a wirkli koa Zeid hod.

2   Deabe Gsatzl

As Boarische strotzt außerdem nur a so voa deabe und umgangssp-
rachliche Gsatzl: Es weard ganz oafach gsogt, wos ma dengt. Und
wenn's nochad dann doch a moi a bisserl deaber nüber kimmt – ja
mei. Und gfluacht weard in Bayern in da Regel a gscheid:

○   Zefix!
○   Ja leck mi am Oarsch!
○   Du Zipfeklatscher!

Mia Bayern san grundsätzlich a soidn friedvolles Voik und wenn
ma uns Beschwern, nachad meistens übas Weda, an Fuaßboi oda
de lokale Politik. Granteln hoaßt im Boarischen schimpfa oder si
beschwern und is a Stigge vo unsana Mentalität. Mia kennan zwar
a amoi gscheid grantig wearn, aba des hoid meist nia recht lang
o. Und de meistn deabn Gsatzl san meist weit weniger schlimm
ois gmoant.

3   Da boarische Konjunktiv

So schene Schimpfwörter und Flüche mia Bayern a ham, mia
kennan a höflich sei! Im Sprachlichen hamma dafür an boarischen

3 Der bayrische Konjunktiv

So schöne Schimpfwörter und Flüche wir Bayern auch haben, wir
können auch höflich sein! Im Sprachlichen sorgt dafür der bayrische Konjunktiv. Manche benutzen und verstehen ihn, andere
benutzen ihn nicht, aber verstehen ihn trotzdem. Und Nicht-Bay-
ern benutzen ihn nicht, und verstehen ihn auch nicht. Was also
ist der bayrische Konjunktiv? Am besten lässt sich das an einem
Beispiel erklären:

- Dadn sie mir den Stui frei hoitn? (dt.: Können Sie mir den
  Stuhl freihalten?)
- I waar jetzad do. (dt.: Ich bin jetzt da.)
- Da Kaffää warad fiate! (dt.: Der Kaffee ist fertig.)

Der bayrische Konjunktiv enthält dabei nicht nur eine offensichtliche Information, sondern auch eine weitere, unterschwellige
Bedeutung. Aus 3. lässt sich beispielsweise nicht nur schließen,
dass der Frühstückskaffee fertig ist, sondern auch, dass die
Frau des Hauses vermutlich bereits genervt und wartend am
Küchentisch sitzt, während sich der Rest der Familie ganz
gemütlich nach und nach einfindet. Diese feine Nuance kann
meisten nur von einem geübten Ohr verstanden und richtig interpretiert werden.

Womit wir auch schon bei einer wichtigen Tatsache wären:
Bayrisch zu sprechen ist leicht, wenn man Muttersprachler ist.
Aufgrund mangelnder Regeln und einer nicht wirklich definierten
Schreibweise der meisten bayrischen Wörter ist der individuellen
Interpretation keine Grenze gesetzt, und das bereitet gerade
Anfängern große Schwierigkeiten. Am besten lernt man Bayern –
sowohl Kultur als auch Sprache – kennen, wenn man etwas Zeit
in der Region verbringt. Die Möglichkeiten sind dabei endlos,

Konjunktiv. Manche nemman'd her und vastengan'd, de andan nemman'd ned her, aba vastengan'd trotzdem. Und Breissn nemman'd ned her und vastengan'd a ned. Wos eiso is da boarische Konjunktiv? Am gscheidsten losst si des an a paar Beispui erklärn:

- Dadn sie mir den Stui frei hoitn?
- I waar jetzad do.
- Da Kaffää warad fiate!

Da boarische Konjunktiv enthoit ned nua a offensichtliche Information, sondern no a andane, unterschwellige Bedeitung. Aus Beispui 3 losst si ned nua schliaßn, dass da Frühstückskaffee fertig is, sondern a, dass de Frau des Hauses vermutlich scho gnervt und wartend am Disch hockt, während da Rest vo da Familie ganz gmiadlich noch und noch einadrudelt. Kloane Nuancen wia de kennan meisten nua von am geübten Ohrwaschel vastandn und gscheid interpretiert wearn.

Womid mia a scho bei ana ganz wichtigen Tatsache warn: Boarisch zum redn is oafach, wenn ma a Muttersprachler is. Wega mangelnder Regeln und ana ned wirklich zu definierenden Schreibweise vo de meistn boarischen Wörta is da individuellen Interpretation koa Grenze gsetzt, und des macht vor allem Anfänger große Schwierigkeiten. Am bestn learnt ma Boarisch – sowohl de Kultur ois a de Sprach' – kenna, wenn ma a bisserl Zeit in da Region vabringt. De Möglichkeiten san dabei endlos, denn Bayern hod ned nur unzählige Brauchdiama und Traditionen zu bietn, sondern a an Haufa Attraktionen und a atemberaubende Natur, vor allem in de Alpen.

Wer Interesse hod, des oa oda andere boarische Woad zum lerna (oda a paar Wörta ausm Artikel nochschaun muas), der soiad si de Vokabellistn in derana Ausgab näher oschaun. Und wenn's Lust denn Bayern hat nicht nur unzählige Bräuche und Traditionen zu bieten, sondern auch eine Vielzahl an Attraktionen und eine atemberaubende Natur, vor allem in den Alpen.

Wenn ihr Lust hast, noch mehr über die bayrische Kultur zu erfahren, dann schaut mal auf die Website von Tongues: Dort habe ich unter dem Titel „Being Bavarian" eine vierteilige Reihe über die bayrische Lebensart verfasst.
In diesem Sinne:

Servus und merce für's Lesen!

*Kleine Anmerkung: Wir Deutschen lieben es, Substantive aneinander zu reihen und zu einem monströsen Wortgebilde zu basteln – das ist auch im Bayrischen nicht anders!

By Ramona Fellermeier

Mia san Mia:
Die einzigartige bayrische Sprache und Kultur

habts, no mehra über de boarische Kultur zum erfoarn, dann schauts moi auf de Website vo Tongues: Do hob i unter dem Titel „Being Bavarian" a fiarteilige Reihe üba de boarische Lebensart gschrimm.

Eiso: Servus und merce fia's Lesn!

The Lioness

by Sukhjit Kaur Khalsa

Sukhjit Kaur Khalsa is a twenty year-old political science and international relations graduate from the University of Western Australia. She is passionate about the performing arts and her pieces are written with the intent to be reworked to perform on stage. Sukhjit, from the age she could pick up a pencil, enjoyed writing and performing scripts to entertain her family. The core themes of these pieces haven't changed since her class clown days and predominantly surround family, stories of the Sikh diaspora and cultural confusions. When she isn't poetry slamming, Sukhjit enjoys creating raps about politics.

"People are like stained-glass windows. They sparkle and shine when the sun is out, but when the darkness sets in, their true beauty is revealed only if there is a light from within."

– Elisabeth Kubler-Ross

What's in a Name?

"Hi, this is Janet ringing from the Heart Foundation. Could I please speak to…Amaaaaar…amooooor…jiiiooot… sorry, how do you pronounce it?"

"Amarjit. Sure, which one…Mr or Mrs?"

"Pardon…?"

"My parents have the same name."

All Sikh names are unisex and have a distinct meaning to them. My name means 'winner of peace'. I know, big shoes to fill, right? I'm no Nelson Mandela or Rosa Parks, but a girl can try.

Apparently, the night before I was born, one of the most destructive storms hit the suburbs of Perth – it swallowed up six hundred homes and left one third of the city in darkness. I like to think of it as Mother Nature throwing me a baby shower, welcoming me into the bosom of her universe. My family, on the other hand, saw it as a warning to the citizens of Western Australia that a wild being was about to thunder into their world.

by Sukhjit Kaur Khalsa

The Lioness

Not only did I thunder into my family's four-place-setting home, but my loudness continues to invade Transperth buses and trains. I've been told to keep the volume down on numerous occasions by people sitting behind me and my friends. Not quite the 'winner of peace' one expects me to be, although it is rather peaceful when I shut up.

Along with being so loud that I've actually been fined for it (while studying abroad in Prague), I have also acquired a bone in my body that itches to advocate for equality – a 'fair go'. Whether it is on the train where a lady in a hijab is told to "take it off" or in a classroom where a boy is bullied for his flamboyancy, I'll be there with my megaphone and picket. Much to my disappointment, I've found people would rather glue themselves to their smartphones than hear my outbursts for justice.

My brother would argue, "Superjet, you're simply a rebel without a cause!"

So here I am, trying to find my cause, my purpose in this world, and my place in the family tree. My ancestry goes back to the war-torn mountain region that borders Pakistan and Afghanistan. My grandparents fled the city of Bannu, which is now located in Pakistan, after the partition of India in 1947. My parents were both born and raised in India, and met three days before their engagement. There was immense pressure from my mother's in-laws to change her name because it was the same as my father's. She refused, so the confusion between their names persists.

The confusion travelled with me to school, where I had an exotic name of my own. My ears would perk up during roll call, when I would hear the almost ritualistic long pause between surnames beginning with 'j' and 'l'.

"Yeah that's me."

"Suck-gjheeet?"
"Suk-i-ji?"
"Suk-a-iit?"
"How about I call you Superjet? It's close enough."

If nothing else, at least my Year Three teacher made me sound
like a superhero. Not all the names given to me were as glorifying.
'Suck-a-shit' was one of my least favourites. The absolute worst,
though, was 'Gorilla Girl'.

Sikh and You Shall Find

We all have our insecurities – mine was my hairy legs. Being
a member of the Sikh faith, we can be recognised by our unshorn
hair and turbans. It gives us a unique identity, and many Sikhs
believe there is a practical and spiritual purpose for every hair on
our body. Brought up in a secluded home away from 'western
influences' and beauty magazines, I grew up believing that Anglo
girls weren't born with leg hair.

I often asked myself: Why aren't I like everybody else? Why don't
I feel feminine?

My questions were usually triggered by advertisements, in which
models would caress their photoshopped legs and exclaim in
voices sweeter than a lotus emerging from my uterus, "Veet: what
beauty feels like".

Am I not a beautiful girl?

by Sukhjit Kaur Khalsa

In the school environment, 'Gorilla Girl' was just one of the forms of verbal abuse I received. I was bullied for four years for not conforming to the high school hierarchy. Every day the number of boys terrorising me grew like an epidemic. As Head Girl of the school it was highly embarrassing.

Instead of throwing a pity party, I decided to twist the traditional bullying victim card. I chose to face all twenty-six of my bullies in a mediated environment. I put them in my shoes and went on to highlight the link between bullying and teenage suicides, racism, hate crimes and current world issues.

"...Most of you guys enjoy playing sport and some of you are in state teams. Imagine you are about to play in a grand final and I rock up with twenty-six of my friends and we start tormenting you from the benches. Deliberately and publicly humiliating you at what you do best. How would that make you feel? Would you be able to perform at your best? I still have the balls to act on stage and do my speeches at assemblies while you chant your little war cries, but there is a tumour inside me. No one deserves that. Not me; not anyone at this school.

"What you are doing is cowardly. Deal with your own shit. Don't use me to get the satisfaction of feeling powerful. If one girl has to stand up to twenty-six of you in front of the principal to be heard, she will. Because I have the guts to face my problems. I abide by our school motto 'Harmony ~ Excellence' and I stay true to the meaning of my name. I am equal to you, whether you like it or not. I deserve to be treated better than that..."

I looked up from my shaky palm cards, after speaking from my heart for forty-five minutes, to find a room filled with a stunned principal, sobbing teachers, speechless friends, and red-faced bullies in tears. As a result, I got an unexpected amount of genuine apologies from the majority of the boys. The day after, the atmosphere changed in the school corridors. No longer did I feel fear or hate. The nods of acknowledgement, smiles and friendly hellos from my bullies made me realise that this opportunity to spread awareness reaped many rewards. Finally, I was a winner of peace. The school was buzzing. Students were finally addressing bullying in a manner that had never, in my experience, been done before. I sent a clear message to my peers: Bring. It. On.

All Sikh boys are given the surname 'Singh' that translates to "Lion" or "King" and all Sikh girls are given the middle or surname 'Kaur' that translates to "Lioness" or "Princess". After accepting my identity as a Sikh and eyeballing bullying right in the face, I rose above a sea of grey. That is the day I took my first steps as a lioness. Now, every day when I leave the house, hairy as ever, I command to the world: Judge Me. I Dare You.

Is hairy the new sexy? Probably not, but I do everything I can to make it the new sexy. With beards growing into fashion, I can't help but wonder when it will be fashionable for women to be hairy.

As I lie on my beach towel and the wind blows through each hair follicle, I feel free. People have often asked me, "How do you deal with people staring at your legs? - 'Cause let's face it, it's not the norm!" My secret is… sunglasses! When I've got my Ray-Bans on, I can pretend not to see the confused I-think-you've-got-fungus-growing-on-your-body-and-I'm-here-to-make-you-aware-of-it look of a passerby. Besides, the stares only last for a couple of seconds until they find something else to judge. My brother once told me, "Sukhjit, your personality should be so exuberant that no one even pays attention to your external looks because they are too in awe of your internal awesomeness".

by Sukhjit Kaur Khalsa

The Lioness

Besides being 'fully-Sikh', you might be curious about who the Sikhs actually are. Before I give you Sikhism101, why don't we take a closer look at what it means to be Australian? Now, I'm not talking about wearing Bintang Beer singlets, eating Vegemite, or being a 'Bogan'. What is the one value that the majority of Australians would share? I'll give you a hint: it starts with M and originated during the World Wars.

Mateship.

Sikhs have come from a divided nation where war and conflict have shaped our identity. Australia is also a nation that began with a colony of convicts and has had to redefine itself, often through international conflict. Australia is a unique nation, one that prides itself on courage and determination. The Australian and Sikh character share a history of struggle that has evolved into a unique 'survivor' mindset.

As humans, we tend to focus on our differences rather than embracing our similarities. Regardless of our race, ethnicity, gender, sexuality, and religion, we are children of the world. When I hear the second chorus of the Australian National Anthem,

"For those who've come across the seas
We've boundless plains to share,
With courage let us all combine
To Advance Australia Fair."

I envision a caring and sharing Australia. An accepting Australia. A handmade Australia. Unfortunately, Australia isn't doing any handholding at the moment; instead, it seems to be doing a lot of 'shooing'.

Indian Accent Sold Separately

I remember applying for one of my first jobs as a 'checkout chick'
at Coles. I rocked up to the front service desk to have a chat and
hand in my résumé. At the counter, I met a colourful character;
a middle-aged Anglo woman wearing old school spectacles,
complete with ropes draping over her sagging ears. Her shiny
badge told me her name was Dorothy. She greeted me with
a grunt of disapproval.

"What can I do for ya, love?"

I began asking whether I could please speak to the manager
regarding a service cashier position. Before I could finish my sentence, Dorothy snatched my résumé and peered at it through the
slit of her glasses, glancing back and forth from the paper to me.
I had started making some casual banter when she blurted out,

"Do you have a visa, honey?"

"...I have a MasterCard?"

"No love, are you illegally in this country? We don't want no illegal
workers here in 'Straya".

I began to chuckle thinking she was cracking a joke, but her
frown lines and obnoxious slowing-down-while-speaking-Eng-
lish-because-you-don't-look 'Strayan tone told me otherwise.
To say I was offended would be an understatement. I grabbed
my résumé and as I walked away I replied, "Perhaps next time,
Dorothy, I should attach an Australian birth certificate to my job
applications."

by Sukhjit Kaur Khalsa

The Lioness

Parallels can be drawn from my experience and a blog post of a Muslim girl living in the United States, who documented a day in which she took off her hijab and the differences in how she was treated by strangers. It was wintertime, so she was still rugged up with a scarf and beanie; covering the same amount of skin that she would normally have covered. This girl described how people acknowledged her presence for the first time and actually smiled at her while passing by. Why was she deprived of this treatment while wearing her cultural attire? She came to the conclusion that "apparently, the type of cloth you place or wrap around your head defines how you will be treated".

I reflect on this by looking inwards at myself. As an adolescent I rarely wore my Indian clothes out in public. Even if we were going to the shops on a Sunday arvo straight after temple, I would refuse to leave the car - mortified that people would see me in my traditional getup and think I was some sort of genie (true story, but we'll get to that later).

My eccentric mother on the other hand, only puts on Western attire for work. The rest of the time, whether door knocking for the Heart Foundation or getting knee high in the beaches of West-'Straya, she'll be flowing in her cultural dress, rocking her colourful prints – loud and proud! She is one of those women who sees a friend in all and genuinely wants to make you laugh. She creeps up on you in the express lane at Woolworths – a lane you chose on purpose – pointing at the glass bottle in your basket, "You might be having chicken tonight, chicken tonight, but I will be making curry tonight, curry tonight". Indian accent sold separately. Whilst out doing her door knocking rounds, she'll ask the most direct, personal and random questions, and then quickly waddle home so she can tell us the gazillion stories about all these new people she met.

"Mum, I don't think the Heart Foundation hired you to do their detective work!"

"They're our neighbours, Sukhjit – if they don't have our back, who vill?"

While I was busy looking 'cool', she was showing the world that you shouldn't be defined by what you wear. Why blend in when you were born to stand out? It's who you are on the inside that really matters. Before you roll your eyes or give me a pitiful nod that says, "awww – bless your cotton socks", hear me out.

These values have derived from my faith. As Sikhs, we stand up for human rights and equality. Sikhism is actually the fifth largest organised religion in the world and not many people have heard of us.

The Turbanator

It is mandatory for Sikh men to wear turbans but it is a choice for Sikh women. The turban is how we crown ourselves as 'Singhs' and 'Kaurs', conveying an identity of royalty, grace, and uniqueness. When you wear a turban, you fearlessly stand out as one single person amongst seven billion.

The turban has had a negative presence in the media ever since the terrorist attacks on the Twin Towers. Since 9/11, Muslims and Sikhs have been victims of hate crimes in the United States, Canada, Europe and Australia. I was still a primary school student in 2001, unaware of the racial divisions that would plant themselves in my neighbourhood and change my perception of Australia. "G'day mate" was replaced with "Go home you terrorist!" and my dad's name, "Amarjit" was replaced with "Osama Bin Laden".

When will I ever be classified as Australian?

These experiences of not belonging led my brother to research the pioneering Sikhs of Western Australia. Shiploads of camels were brought to Australia in the 1860s for transport and construction as part of the colonisation of the central and western parts of the country. Among the handlers of the camels were some Sikhs. Sikhs were mistakenly called Afghans as the term 'Afghan' was used for any dark-skinned turbaned person, especially if he was a cameleer or a hawker. We discovered that Sikhs have actually been around in Western Australia for over one hundred and fifty years. It's hilarious when someone tells my family to go home to where we came from because now I simply tell them: "We've been right at home for the past one hundred and fifty years, mate."

I don't really have a distinct physical identity as a Sikh because my hairiness seems to pass off as "feminist", or "lesbian" or "just another hairy Indian". However, I still feel the need to fight these injustices even though they don't directly affect me. I feel attached to the firsthand racism Sikh men receive. When they experience a hate crime, I feel as though I have experienced a hate crime.

In January 2014 I decided to start wearing a turban. It ended up being an unintentional social experiment. What was the big hoohaa about the struggle of a Sikh male? Was it really that alienating to wear a turban? Funnily enough, I received more prejudice from my own Sikh community than the wider Australian public. As a Sikh girl, wearing a turban challenges the beliefs of others. Everyone had an opinion and I became a hot topic on 'The Great Sikh Debate of Perth'.

"Why is she wearing that thing on her head? Great, now
she's gone all religious on us."

"So proud of her, she is finally showing us she is a religious girl.
Hang on – why is she still showing off her skin?"

"Don't go around throwing your turban in my face, you fundamen-
talist!"

"Did you see her talking to that man? A turbaned girl must be
modest at all times!"

"Her poor mother, no one will want to marry her daughter! She will
die making curry for one!"

"Ew, hairy AND a turban! I like my Sikh girls skanky! Unless it's in
front of my parents, then she'd better cover up!"

"Bro, she seems like the perfect girl for me now. Religious AND
modern! Thank God she doesn't have any facial hair though!"

"Who does she think she is? Equality between men and women?
She can take her feminist beliefs elsewhere!"

Through this experience I learnt we are not just our beliefs. A Muslim
woman is not just her hijab. Quite like a nun is not just her robe or
a police officer is not just their uniform, I am not just my turban. I am
not just my hair. I am Sukhjit – evolving through my life experiences
and hopefully getting closer to the actual intention of my name.

You might be wondering how everyday Australians reacted to
'The Turbanator'?
They didn't. That's how.

The Lioness

by Sukhjit Kaur Khalsa

Generally in Australia we tend to ignore the elephant in the room. The great thing about kids, though, is that they don't ignore the elephant – they jump right on and ask for a ride. I was sitting on the train on my way to university, when a toddler sitting on the seat opposite me pointed excitedly and said, "Look Mum, a genie! A genie! It's a GENIE!!!!!!" I chuckled. His mum went bright red and pretended I wasn't even there. I thought, lady – your son said genie, not ghost!

Before his mum could stop him, he ran up to my seat greeting me with his beaming wide eyes, "Genie, can you grant me three wishes?" As he went on to list what he wanted, I thought to myself, we are not born racist; we are taught these differences from a young age. My wish for the future is that people will learn to see the inner beauty in all. Then maybe we can all be winners of peace.

You look like a million dollars!

Wyglądać jak milion dolarów!

American Influence on Polish Culture Reflected in Language

Amerykańskie wpływy na polską kulturę i ich odzwierciedlenie w języku

By Dr. Joanna Szerszunowicz

Joanna Szerszunowicz is a graduate of Polish philology and English philology with a doctorate in Contrastive Linguistics, currently employed at the University of Białystok, Poland, as an Assistant Professor. She teaches Contrastive Phraseology, Practical Stylistics and Linguistics. The focal issues of her reasearch are: phraseology (Polish, English and Italian faunal phraseology, Polish, English and Italian onymic phraseology; culture-boundness of phraseological units, phraseological gaps in a contrastive perspective), linguo-cultural studies of lexis and phraseolgy, translation, mono- and bilingual phraseography, teaching Polish as a mother tongue and a foreign language and teaching English as a foreign language.

Poland is a country with a long and turbulent history of many wars, uprisings and three partitions. Erased from the world map to finally regain independence, it is an ethnic community influenced by several cultures, which are reflected in its language. For instance, an analysis of the borrowings, which have enriched the Polish lexicon over centuries, shows how historical events and cultural background are reflected in the language. Old loan words include Greek, Latin, Turkish, French, Italian, German, Russian, and Ukrainian lexical items, while the newer ones come mostly from English. Nowadays, similarly to many other countries, Poland is exposed to the American influence in many areas: science, economy and entertainment, to name but a few. The aim of the article is to discuss how this impact is reflected in the Polish language.

America on the Polish mental map

Many place names are carriers of stereotypical images, i.e. conventionalised pictures, functioning in a given culture[1]. Such pictures of various places – both big and recognised internationally and small, known locally because of some particular reason – constitute the mental map of the world[2], shared by those belonging to a given ethnic community, for instance, Poles. The knowledge of such a map is necessary to understand and interpret various texts of a given language: press articles, literature, commercials and many others. The images of places may contain

---

1   The term culture is one of the most important in humanities and it has many definitions. In the present paper, Alfred Weber's definition is adopted, according to which culture starts where life needs finish, it means it is above them and includes values, beliefs, ideologies, group lifestyles, science and art. A. Weber, Ideen zur Staats- und Kultursoziologie, G. Braun, Karlsruhe 1927. For an overview of definitions see Alfred L. Kroeber, Clyde Kluckhohn, Culture. A Critical Review of Concepts and Definitions, Peabody Museum, Cambridge Mass. 1952.

2   Wojciech Chlebda. 2002. Polak przed mentalną mapą świata [A Pole in front of a mental map of the world]. Etnolingwistyka 14, pp. 9-26.

By Dr. Joanna Szerszunowicz

Polska jest krajem o długiej i pełnej zawirowań historii, w której było wiele wojen i trzy rozbiory. To państwo, które znikało z mapy świata, aby w końcu odzyskać niepodległość. Na tę wspólnotę etniczną miało wpływ wiele kultur, co znajduje odzwierciedlenie w języku. Przykładowo, analiza zapożyczeń, które przez wieki wzbogacały polskie słownictwo, pokazuje, jak wydarzenia historyczne i uwarunkowania kulturowe wpływają na język. Dawne zapożyczenia pochodzą z takich języków, jak grecki, łaciński, turecki, francuski, włoski, niemiecki, rosyjski i ukraiński. Nowsze pochodzą zaś przede wszystkim z angielskiego. W obecnych czasach, podobnie do wielu innych krajów, Polska pozostaje pod wpływami Ameryki w wielu obszarach, wśród których warto wymienić chociażby naukę, gospodarkę czy rozrywkę. Celem artykułu jest przedstawienie, jakie są przejawy tych wpływów w języku polskim.

Ameryka na mentalnej mapie Polaków

Wiele nazw miejscowych to nośniki wyobrażeń stereotypowych, czyli skonwencjonalizowanych obrazów funkcjonujących w danej kulturze[1]. Takie wizerunki różnych miejsc – zarówno dużych, znanych na arenie międzynarodowej, jak i małych, kojarzonych z czymś lokalnie – tworzą mentalną mapę świata[2], wspólną ludziom należącym do określonej wspólnoty etnicznej, na przykład Polakom. Znajomość takiej mapy jest niezbędna do rozumienia

---

1   Termin kultura jest jednym z najważniejszych w naukach humanistycznych i ma wiele definicji. W niniejszym artykule przyjęto definicję Alfred Webera, głoszącą, że kultura zaczyna się tam, gdzie kończą się potrzeby życiowe, co oznacza, że jest ona ponad nimi i obejmuje wartości, poglądy, ideologie, grupowe style życia, naukę i sztukę. A. Weber, Ideen zur Staats- und Kultursoziologie, G. Braun, Karlsruhe 1927. Przegląd definicji zawiera: Alfred L. Kroeber, Clyde Kluckhohn, Culture. A Critical Review of Concepts and Definitions, Peabody Museum, Cambridge Mass. 1952.

2   Wojciech Chlebda. 2002. Polak przed mentalną mapą świata. Etnolingwistyka 14, s. 9-26.

both objective characteristics (e.g. The USA is a big country) as well as the ones attributed to a given place by a particular nation (e.g. The USA is an attractive country to live in).

One of the axes of this map, especially important for Polish culture, is the geographical opposition of the West and the East. The location of Poland was described by a Polish dramatist, writer and cartoonist Sławomir Mrożek in the following way: *A country which is to the east of the West and to the west of the East*[3]. Both areas developed conventional images in Polish culture. The former, West, is perceived as the culture and civilisation centre, a bastion of stability, democracy and wealth, opposed to the latter, East, associated with poverty and aggression[4]. In general, the West tends to be considered by the Polish to be offering its inhabitants more than their own country and the East do.

Therefore, in the Polish collective memory, the general picture of the USA, classified as a Western country, remains positive. Polish emigration has had a long tradition, which contributes to the stability of the good image of the country. It is perceived by the vast majority of Poles as a land of opportunities, the "promised land", where the "American dream" can come true, "the sky is the limit" and everybody can be successful if they try hard, irrespective of their origins, beliefs and religion.

In 1922, in the introduction to his translation of Prentice Mulford's novel, Stanisław Michalski wrote: "From America, the country of dollar, humbug and commercials came the strange

---

3   The quotation is taken from S. Mrożek's play titled Kontrakt, published in 1986. All translations in the article own.

4   Jerzy Bartmiński, Miejsce wartości w językowym obrazie świata [The place of values in a linguistic picture of the world], in idem, Językowe podstawy obrazu świata, Wydawnictwo UMCS, Lublin 2006, p. 140.

American Influence on Polish Culture
Reflected in Language

i interpretowania rozmaitych tekstów w danym języku: artykułów prasowych, literatury, reklamy i wielu innych. Omawiane wyobrażenia miejsc mogą zawierać cechy obiektywne (np. USA to duży kraj) oraz przypisane nazywanemu miejscu przez daną narodowość (np. USA jest atrakcyjnym krajem).

Jedną z osi tej mapy, szczególnie ważną dla kultury polskiej, jest geograficzna opozycja Wschód – Zachód. Dramatopisarz, prozaik i rysownik Sławomir Mrożek określił położenie Polski w następujący sposób: *Kraj, który położony jest na wschód od Zachodu i na zachód od Wschodu*[3]. Oba te obszary mają ustalone wyobrażenia w kulturze polskiej: pierwszy z nich, Zachód, jest postrzegany jako centrum kultury i cywilizacji, bastion stabilności, demokracji i dobrobytu, w przeciwieństwie do drugiego z nich, Wschodu, kojarzonego z biedą i agresją[4]. Ogólnie ujmując, Polacy uważają, że kraje zachodnie oferują więcej swoim mieszkańcom niż te położone na Wschodzie.

Z tego powodu w pamięci zbiorowej Polaków utrwalił się pozytywny obraz USA, kraju klasyfikowanego jako zachodni. Wizerunek ten jest względnie stabilny, utrzymuje się bowiem w zasadniczo niezmienionej postaci od wielu lat. Polska emigracja ma długą tradycję, co przyczynia się do utrzymania takiego obrazu przez Stany Zjednoczone. Są one postrzeganego przez większość Polaków jako kraj sposobności, „ziemia obiecanej", gdzie "niebo wyznacza granicę" i spełnia się „American dream" – każdy może bowiem odnieść sukces, jeśli pracuje ciężko, niezależnie od pochodzenia, poglądów i religii.

---

3   Cytat pochodzi z sztuki S. Mrożka pod tytułem Kontrakt, opublikowanej w 1986. Wszystkie tłumaczenia w artykule własne.

4   Jerzy Bartmiński, Miejsce wartości w językowym obrazie świata, in idem, Językowe podstawy obrazu świata, Wydawnictwo UMCS, Lublin 2006, s. 140.

and beautiful book to us. From the country of wild fever of life,
never-satiable appetites and desires, from the country of low
instincts, and at the same time one of iron will, work and energy,
from the country of the richest, more and more powerful univer-
sities, from the new, big country, full democratic society (...)"[5].
Although the sentences were written a long time ago, most of his
observations regarding America are identical or similar to contemporary Poles' opinions on the place[6].

The USA is constantly perceived as a powerful country with
a strong economy, multiethnic and multiracial, welcoming those
who believe in hard work as the key to being successful. The
image of the country fostered the development of the stereotypical picture of an American in Polish culture. The conventionalised
picture of a representative of this nation is composed of such
characteristics as being rich, self-confident, enterprising, relaxed
and easy-going. These features comply with many – especially
young – Poles' systems of values[7]. Therefore, in various contexts
the Polish nouns *Ameryka* and *Amerykanin* as well as the adjec-
tive *amerykański* ('American') evoke positive associations.

Anglo-American influence on the Polish language and culture

After the statehood transformation, which took place in 1989,
Poland changed its political system and adopted a free market
economy. It was then that many foreign companies set up their

---

5   The excerpt from the introduction written by the translator of the novel. Prentice Mulford, Przeciw śmierci, translation and introduction by S. Michalski, Trzaska, Evert i Michalski, Warszawa 1922, p. 5.

6   Kazimierz Ożóg, Atrakcyjna amerykanizacja w kulturze i języku polskim [At-
tractive Americanness in culture and in the Polish language], in idem, Polszczyzna
przełomu XX i XXI wieku. Wybrane zagadnienia, Fraza, Rzeszów 2001, pp. 224-
238.

7   Ibidem, p.141.

W opublikowanym w 1922 roku wstępie do tłumaczenia powieści Prentice'a Mulforda Stanisław Michalski napisał: "Z Ameryki, kraju dolara, humbugu i reklamy przyszła do nas ta dziwna i piękna książka. Z kraju wściekłej gorączki życiowej, nienasyconych nigdy pożądań i apetytów, z kraju najniższych namiętności, lecz jednocześnie żelaznej woli, pracy i energji, z kraju korupcji, trustów, Tamany-Hall – i jednocześnie z kraju najbogatszych, coraz potężniejszych uniwersytetów, z kraju nowego, olbrzymiego, nawskróś demokratycznego społeczeństwa (...)"[5]. Chociaż te zdania pochodzą sprzed wielu lat, większość z zawartych w nich obserwacji dotyczących Ameryki stanowią spostrzeżenia w dużym stopniu zbieżne z opiniami współcześnie żyjących Polaków[6].

Stany Zjednoczone cały czas postrzegane są jako mocarstwo z silną ekonomią, wieloetniczne i wielorasowe, przyjmujące chętnie tych, którzy wierzą, że ciężka praca jest kluczem do sukcesu. Taki obraz był podstawą ukształtowania stereotypu Amerykanina w kulturze polskiej. Na skonwencjonalizowane wyobrażenie przedstawiciela tej narodowości składają się następujące elementy: bycie bogatym, pewność siebie, przedsiębiorczość, pozytywne podejście do życia i bezproblemowość. Te cechy pasują do systemu wartości Polaków, zwłaszcza młodego pokolenia[7]. Z tego powodu w wielu rozmaitych kontekstach polskie rzeczowniki *Ameryka* i *Amerykanin* oraz przymiotnik *amerykański* wywołują pozytywne skojarzenia.

---

5   Przytoczony fragment, w którym zachowano pisownię, pochodzi ze wstępu od tłumacza przełożonego na język angielski. Prentice Mulford, Przeciw śmierci, wstęp i tłumaczenie S. Michalski, Trzaska, Evert i Michalski, Warszawa 1922, s. 5.

6   Kazimierz Ożóg, Atrakcyjna amerykanizacja w kulturze i języku polski , in idem, Polszczyzna przełomu XX i XXI wieku. Wybrane zagadnienia, Fraza, Rzeszów 2001, s. 224-238.

7   Ibidem, s.141.

branches in Poland and Poles started to travel abroad frequently, which resulted in more contact with foreigners. The influence of the English language on Polish increased significantly within a short period of time, especially between 1985 and 1994[8], and this trend continues today.

It has manifested itself clearly in lexis: many borrowings have appeared, especially in areas, either not present in the Polish communist past, such as marketing, or have developed, for instance, business (*biznesplan* [business plan], *menedżer* [manager], *marketing* [marketing]) and technology (*komputer* [computer], *modem* [modem], *walkman* [walkman]). Many loans filled in lexical gaps naming various new phenomena, for example, *komputer* [computer], *modem* [modem], *snowboard* [snowboard] and *cartridż* [cartridge].

It is worth noting the presence of prestige loans from English in the Polish language, i.e. words or phrases not needed, but adopted, since foreign words, especially English, were considered more prestigious. Good examples in case are the following words: *loft* ('loft'), *designerski* ('designer's'), *cool* ('cool'). The words at issue tend to be used as elements of image creation, for example, by celebrities. Moreover, English, now commonly taught at all levels of education in Polish schools, is common in youth jargon[9], with many loans such as *wow* or *sorry*.

---

8   A steady increase has been observed: up to 1961 – over 700 anglicisms (incorporated since 18th c.), then respectively: 1985 – about 300, up to 1994 – about 600. Elżbieta Mańczak-Wohlfeld, Angielskie elementy leksykalne w języku polskim [English lexical elements in the Polish language], Universitas, Kraków 1994, p. 8.

9   Generally speaking, English has a big influence on the language of young Poles. See Agnieszka Otwinowska-Kasztelanic, A study of lexico-semantic and grammatical influence of English on the Polish of the younger generation of Poles (19-35 years of age), Wydawnictwo Akademickie DIALOG, Warszawa 2000.

American Influence on Polish Culture
Reflected in Language

By Dr. Joanna Szerszunowicz

Angloamerykański wpływ na język i kulturę w Polsce

Po transformacji ustrojowej, która miała miejsce w 1989 roku, w Polsce zmienił się system polityczny i przyjęto zasady gospodarki wolnorynkowej. Wtedy wiele zagranicznych firm założyło filie w Polsce, a Polacy zaczęli częściej podróżować, co zaowocowało licznymi kontaktami z obcokrajowcami. Oddziaływanie języka angielskiego na polszczyznę wzrosło znacznie w krótkim okresie, zwłaszcza w latach 1985-1994[8]. Tendencja ta utrzymuje się do dnia dzisiejszego.

Wpływy angielszczyzny najbardziej widoczne są w słownictwie: pojawiło się wiele zapożyczeń, przede wszystkim w obszarach nieobecnych w realiach Polski socjalistycznej, takich jak marketing, lub tych, które były słabo rozwinięte, na przykład business (*biznesplan*, *menedżer*, *marketing*) i technologii (*komputer*, *modem*, *walkman*). Wiele zapożyczeń wypełniło luki leksykalne, nazywając nowe zjawiska, przedmioty itp. Takimi wyrazami są na przykład słowa *komputer*, *modem*, *snowboard* czy *cartridż*.

Warto wspomnieć o istnieniu w języku polskim angielskich zapożyczeń o charakterze prestiżowym, czyli takich słów i wyrażeń, które nie były niezbędne z punktu widzenia komunikacji, ale zostały przyjęte, ponieważ ich angielskie brzmienie odbiera się jako atrakcyjne i nadające wypowiedzi prestiż. Należą do nich między innymi następujące słowa: *loft*, *designerski*, *cool*. Omawiane wyrazy wykorzystywane są jako element budowania własnego wizerunku, na przykład przez znane osoby. Ponadto język angielski, powszechnie nauczany w szkołach na wszystkich poziomach,

---

8 Stopniowy wzrost liczby zapożyczeń z języka angielskiego: do 1961 – ponad 700 anglicyzmów (zasilających zasób słownictwo od XVIII w.), następnie: do 1985 – około 300, do 1994 – około 600. Elżbieta Mańczak-Wohlfeld, Angielskie elementy leksykalne w języku polskim, Universitas, Kraków 1994, s. 8.

Lexical loans are easy to notice, even for those language users who are not linguists. However, a multiaspectual analysis of language-culture relations gives an insight into the real extent of the American influence on Polish culture. Thanks to such research, it is possible to discuss American culture related changes observed in other areas, such as communication patterns or the system of values, and their reflection in the language.

Generally speaking, American culture favours informality. This preference can be observed in many spheres: casual clothes, hair style, nude makeup, ways of behaving and addressing people. In terms of interpersonal communication, a short distance between speakers is perfectly acceptable, especially with the universal *you* forms. The addressative system of Polish culture differentiates between the formal forms (either *pan* [Mister], *pani* [Mrs/Ms/Miss] + the 3rd person singular or państwo [Mister and Mrs/Ms/Miss] + the 3rd person plural) and the informal ones (ty [you] + the 2nd person singular or wy [you] + the 2nd person plural). There are also semi-formal forms, like pan/pani [Mister/Mrs/Ms/Miss] followed by the first name. What is important is the fact that changing the pan/pani form to you results in making the relation between people closer.

Nowadays, in the Polish culture, there is a growing preference for informal forms. It can be attributed to the American way of conversation observed in films and in direct contact with Americans. Using the ty [you] form or first names instead of the traditional pan/pani [Sir/Madam] is very common in press interviews as well as in radio and television programs, even if the host meets the interviewee for the first time. It is worth adding that people working in show business started to use short forms of their names in a formal context, for instance, Kuba [Jimmy] Wojewódzki instead of Jakub [James] Wojewódzki. This practice had been consid-

By Dr. Joanna Szerszunowicz

American Influence on Polish Culture
Reflected in Language

jest obecny w żargonie młodzieżowym[9]. Występuje w nim wiele zapożyczeń, wśród których znajdujemy takie elementy leksykalne jak *wow* czy *sorry*.

Angielskie zapożyczenia leksykalne łatwo jest zauważyć nawet tym, którzy nie zajmują się zawodowo językiem. Jednak wieloaspektowa analiza językowo-kulturowych związków pokazuje, jaki jest prawdziwy zakres amerykańskich wpływów na kulturę polską. Szersze spojrzenie na tę kwestię pozwala na wychwycenie zmian uwarunkowanych oddziaływaniem kultury amerykańskiej, występujących w schematach komunikacji czy w językowym odzwierciedleniu systemu wartości.

Ogólnie mówiąc, w kulturze amerykańskiej ważną kategorią jest bezpośredniość i luz, co obserwuje się w wielu obszarach: nieoficjalnym stylu ubierania i czesania się, naturalnym makijażu, sposobie bycia i zwracania się do ludzi. W kategoriach komunikacji interpersonalnej mały dystans między rozmówcami jest w pełni akceptowany, czemu sprzyja uniwersalna forma *you*. System adresatywny polszczyzny zakłada rozróżnienie form oficjalnych (*pan, pani* + 3 os. lp. lub *państwo* + 3 os. l.mn.) i nieoficjalnych (*ty* + 2 os. l.poj. lub *wy* + 2 os. l.mn.). Występują również formy pośrednie, na przykład konstrukcja *pan/pani* w połączeniu z imieniem. Zmiana formy z *pan, pani* na *ty* oznacza zmianę statusu rozmówcy i jest oznaką zacieśnienia relacji między ludźmi.

Obecnie w kulturze polskiej obserwuje się wyraźny wzrost preferencji dla form nieoficjalnych. Może w tym upatrywać wpływów amerykańskiego stylu konwersacyjnego oglądanego na filmach

9   Ogólnie ujmując, angielszczyzna ma duży wpływ na język młodych Polaków. Zob. Agnieszka Otwinowska-Kasztelanic, A study of lexico-semantic and grammatical influence of English on the Polish of the younger generation of Poles (19-35 years of age), Wydawnictwo Akademickie DIALOG, Warszawa 2000.

ered unusual before 1989 and even nowadays is rather limited to show business and a few public persons who opt for such forms. Generally speaking, accepting informality of communication is perceived as an attractive quality of the speaker, showing that a given person is friendly and open.

Being positive, an expression of friendliness, is another important characteristic of American culture, attested by many sayings, proverbs and pragmatic idioms. The communication scenario includes the element of being nice to others, which is observed in numerous phrases of pragmatic character, such as *How nice to see you!*, *Nice to meet you!*, *It will be nice to meet up!*, *Have a nice day!*, *Have a nice weekend!* etc. Although it can be assumed that the quality of being nice can be treated as universal and close to politeness, it should be emphasised that politeness is a culture-related notion. Thus, one can expect that American and Polish perceptions of politeness will differ.

It is confirmed by the fact that the Polish expression *Życzę miłego dnia!*, a translation of the English phrase *Have a nice day!*, is a relatively recent borrowing. First, it was used by sales persons, insurance agents etc., who were taught to use it during workshops modelled on those in American companies. Then the phrase became widely popular, with many variants, such as *Miłego popołudnia!*, *Miłego wieczoru!*, *Miłego weekendu!*. Although such units can be treated as exponents of politeness – they warm up relations between people, including those who do not know each other – they are not part of the Polish tradition. Because of it, linguists, especially those setting norms, advise that such forms should be used by professionals rendering services, like bank clerks, shop assistants or hairdressers[10]. As already mentioned,

---

10   Małgorzata Marcjanik, Grzeczność w komunikacji językowej [Politeness in language communication], Wydawnictwo Naukowe PWN, Warszawa 2007, pp. 53-54.

By Dr. Joanna Szerszunowicz

i jego obserwacji w bezpośrednich kontaktach z Amerykanami. Używanie formy *ty* lub mówienie sobie po imieniu zamiast stosowania tradycyjnej formy *pan/pani* staje się coraz częstsze w wywiadach prasowych oraz programach radiowych i telewizyjnych, nawet jeśli rozmówcy spotykają się po raz pierwszy. Wart dodać, że ludzie show businessu zaczęli używać zdrobniałych form imion w sytuacjach oficjalnych, na przykład Kuba Wojewódzki zamiast Jakub Wojewódzki. Przed 1989 rokiem wykorzystywanie zdrobnień w taki sposób zdarzało się sporadycznie i nawet w dzisiejszych czasach ograniczone jest do kręgu ludzi pracujących w sferze rozrywki oraz kilku osób publicznych, które zdecydowały się na posługiwanie taką wersją imienia. Uogólniając, brak oficjalności w procesie komunikacji jest postrzegany jako atrakcyjna cecha mówiącego, świadcząca o jego otwartości i przyjaznym podejściu do drugiego człowieka.

Pozytywne nastawienie do ludzi i świata jest kolejną ważną cechą kultury amerykańskiej, co ma poświadczenie w wielu powiedzeniach, przysłowiach i idiomach pragmatycznych. Scenariusz komunikacyjny zakłada wyrażanie pozytywnego stosunku do innych, do czego służą liczne wyrażenia i zwroty, takie jak: *How nice to see you!*, *Nice to meet you!*, *It will be nice to meet up! Have a nice day!*, *Have a nice weekend!* itp. Chociaż można przyjąć założenie, że bycie miłym dla rozmówców ma charakter uniwersalny, ponieważ wiąże się z uprzejmością, należy podkreślić, że uprzejmość ma uwarunkowania kulturowe, a zatem amerykańskie i polskie rozumienie uprzejmości będzie się różnić.

Potwierdzenie różnic kulturowych stanowi fakt, że polskie wyrażenie *Życzę miłego dnia!*, tłumaczenie angielskiego *Have a nice day!*, to stosunkowo nowe zapożyczenie. Początkowo było ono używane przez sprzedawców itp., którzy przyswoili je podczas warsztatów prowadzonych na wzór tych, jakie są organizowane irrespective of such recommendations, the phrase *Have a nice day* and its variants are widely used by Poles, both persons who are on friendly terms and those who are not really familiar with each other.

In general, Poles try to sound positive, which is in line with the American standard. In the Polish communication model, complaining has always been acceptable. It is considered to be part of the autostereotype. Even after a short stay in Poland, many foreigners comment on the Polish tendency to complain, perceived as "being always negative about everything". Historically conditioned inclination to complain is another element which has been influenced by the American life philosophy, which is well reflected in language, for instance, by the slogan *The sky is the limit*, the phrase *Keep smiling* or the idiom *from rags to riches*.

Sounding positive started to be a desired quality in people, which can be observed in small talk conversations. Generally speaking, there is more truth value in Polish small talk than in American small talk. Therefore, depending on the speakers' familiarity, the question meaning How are you? can be interpreted by Poles as a real question or as a polite phrase, similar to a greeting. It means that the Polish small talk formula allows for presenting things as they are, even telling others about one's problems. It is well manifested in an idiomatic answer to such questions – *Stare biedy,* which literally means 'old problems' or 'old worries'. However, nowadays being optimistic and friendly is more and more common in such dialogues, whereas complaining, considered to be part of the Polish traditional discourse, occurs less frequently[11].

---

11   Joanna Szerszunowicz, A Comparative Analysis of Small Talk in English and Polish. In Theoretical Approaches to Dialogue Analysis. Selected Papers from the IADA Chicago 2004 Conference, ed. L. N. Berlin, Niemeyer, Tübingen 2007, pp. 39-48.

American Influence on Polish Culture
Reflected in Language

w korporacjach amerykańskich, później zyskało ono dużą popularność. W polszczyźnie istnieją jego liczne warianty *Miłego popołudnia! Miłego wieczoru! Miłego weekendu!* Chociaż takie jednostki są traktowane jako wykładniki grzeczności, ocieplające relacje między ludźmi, również tymi nieznającymi się nawzajem, nie należą one do polskiej tradycji. Z tego powodu językoznawcy zajmujący się poprawnością językową i obowiązującymi normami, zalecają, aby takich form używały osoby świadczące usługi, na przykład urzędnicy bankowi, ekspedienci i fryzjerzy[10]. Jak już wspomniano, niezależnie od zaleceń specjalistów Polacy często używają wyrażenia *Have a nice day* i jego wariantów. Posługują się nimi zarówno ci, którzy dobrze się znają, jak i osoby nieznajome.

Uogólniając, Polacy starają się nadać swoim wypowiedziom pozytywny ton, co jest zgodne ze standardem amerykańskim. W polskiej komunikacji narzekanie było powszechnie akceptowane i traktowane jako element autostereotypu. Nawet po krótkim pobycie w Polsce wielu obcokrajowców zauważa, że Polacy mają tendencję do „negatywnego nastawienia do wszystkiego". Historycznie uwarunkowana skłonność do narzekania uległa zmianie pod wpływem amerykańskiej filozofii życiowej, zawartej w takich wyrażeniach jak *The sky is the limit, Keep smiling* czy *from rags to riches.*

Bycie pozytywnym zaczęło być dobrze widziane w polskim społeczeństwie, co znajduje to odzwierciedlenie w codziennych rozmowach. Generalizując, można powiedzieć, że polskie dialogi tego rodzaju zakładają większy stopień szczerości. Z tego powodu w zależności od stopnia znajomości rozmówców pytanie *Jak się masz?* może być zinterpretowane przez Polaków jako prawdziwe pytanie lub jako wyrażenie grzecznościowe podobne do

---

10   Małgorzata Marcjanik, Grzeczność w komunikacji językowej,
Wydawnictwo Naukowe PWN, Warszawa 2007, s. 53-54.

Sending positive messages is an important element of self-image construction, as it builds a picture of a nice and successful person.

Success is another key word in defining changes in Polish culture after 1989. The new model of economy, based on free market rules, favours those determined to succeed. In order to be successful one needs to compete with others and be better than their competitors. Therefore, everything is important in this struggle: hard skills, emotional intelligence and also looks. The American saying *Dress makes success* also stresses the importance of good looks. As for Polish proverbs and sayings, they reflect two views of looks: the first one stresses the lack of importance of appearance (*Nie szata zdobi człowieka* [The dress does not make a person beautiful]), the other expresses the opposite and its meaning is similar to the American saying (*Jak cię widzą, tak cię piszą* [They evaluate you according to how they see you]).

In the Polish language there are fixed expressions used for describing persons who look good. Many of them are fossilised comparisons, which refer to a supernatural or real entity epitomising beauty. Among them there are phrases describing women: *wyglądać jak anioł* [to look like an angel], *wyglądać jak bóstwo* [to look like a deity], *wyglądać jak królewna* [to look like a queen], *wyglądać jak księżniczka* [to look like a duchess], and two phrases used about handsome men: *wyglądać jak panisko* [to look like a lord] and *wyglądać jak młody bóg* [to look like a young god]. Several phrases are based on textual or pictorial images, like *wyglądać jak z bajki* [to look like one is from a fairy tale], *wyglądać jak z obrazka* [to look like one is from a picture], *wyglądać jak z żurnala* [to look like one is from a fashion magazine][12].

---

12   Mirosław Bańko, Słownik porównań [Dictionary of similes], Wydawnictwo Naukowe PWN, Warszawa 2004, pp. 189-190.

American Influence on Polish Culture
Reflected in Language

powitania. Oznacza to, że polski model codziennych rozmów dopuszcza szczerość, a więc nawet dzielenie się z rozmówcami problemami. Językowy ślad omawianej kwestii znajdujemy w postaci stałego połączenia wyrazowego *Stare biedy*, używanego jako odpowiedź na omawiane pytanie. Jednak należy podkreślić, że współcześnie wyrażanie pozytywnego nastawienia jest w takich dialogach coraz częstsze, podczas gdy narzekanie, uważane za element polskiej tradycji, występuje rzadziej[11]. Wysyłanie pozytywnych komunikatów to ważny element budowania własnego wizerunku jako osoby przyjaznej i odnoszącej sukcesy w różnych dziedzinach.

Sukces to kolejne słowo definiujące zmiany, które zaszły w polskiej kulturze po 1989 roku. Nowy model gospodarki, oparty na zasadach wolnego rynku, sprzyja tym, którzy zdecydowani są pracować ciężko. Odnoszenie sukcesów wymaga podjęcia rywalizacji z innymi i bycia od nich lepszym. W tej walce wszystko jest więc ważne: umiejętności twarde, inteligencja emocjonalna, a także wygląd. Amerykańskie powiedzenie *Dress makes success* również podkreśla znaczenie wizerunku zewnętrznego. Polskie przysłowia i powiedzenia odzwierciedlają dwa poglądy dotyczące tej kwestii: pierwsze z nich zwraca uwagę na małe znaczenie wyglądu (*Nie szata zdobi człowieka*), drugie zaś wyraża przeciwne znaczenie i jest bliskie amerykańskiemu (*Jak cię widzą, tak cię piszą*).

W polszczyźnie występuje wiele stałych połączeń opisujących osoby, które są atrakcyjne. Wiele z nich to porównania, w których piękna osoba zestawiana jest z prawdziwą lub wyimaginowaną istotą stanowiącą uosobienie piękna, na przykład frazeologizmy opisujące kobiety – *wyglądać jak anioł, wyglądać jak bóstwo, wy-*

---

11   Joanna Szerszunowicz, A Comparative Analysis of Small Talk in English and Polish. In Theoretical Approaches to Dialogue Analysis. Selected Papers from the IADA Chicago 2004 Conference, ed. L. N. Berlin, Niemeyer, Tübingen 2007, s. 39-48.

As it can be seen, among Polish idioms and proverbs there are no phrases referring to money, whereas the English fixed comparison *to look like a million dollars* employs such imagery. In Polish, a phrase with a substituted constituent, i.e. using the Polish currency (złoty), *wyglądać jak milion złotych*, sounds surprising, even strange – comparing good looks to money seems to be unusual and inappropriate. Rooted deeply in the Protestant faith, the American belief in working hard and being rewarded for it, also in financial terms, may give an insight into the possible foundations of the metaphor. The evaluation of earning money and possessing is positive, while in Poland, especially during the communist times, being wealthy was associated with being a party dignitary or being dishonest. Poles' perceptions of earning money have changed since the relatively recent statehood transformation, yet in Polish the metaphor is absent.

Irrespective of the fact, the English loan phrase *wyglądać jak milion dolarów*, using dollars instead of złoty, started to be used and is becoming more and more popular, mostly in press texts, in particular in those published on the Internet. It can be found in articles, especially those on celebrities, in demotivators and many others. The phrase can be classified as a borrowing which, on one hand, reflects the cultural changes, consistent in perceiving good looks as an important element of evaluation, for instance at job interviews, and, which, on the other, thanks to its widespread nature, promotes the new viewpoint. Undeniably, it is attractive because of novelty, but one can also suppose that, similarly to the phrases discussed before, it reflects changes in Poles' viewpoints. New comparisons are possible, because the reality is different: the modern culture after 1989 evaluates highly any kind of success, including financial achievements. Therefore, the acceptance of a phrase *you look like a million dollars* translated into Polish is easier than before.

By Dr. Joanna Szerszunowicz

American Influence on Polish Culture
Reflected in Language

glądać jak królewna, *wyglądać jak księżniczka*, oraz dwa związki wyrazowe używane w stosunku do mężczyzn: *wyglądać jak panisko* i *wyglądać jak młody bóg*. Język polski ma również w swoim zasobie połączenia odnoszące się do skonwencjonalizowanych wyobrażeń tekstów kulturowych, na przykład: *wyglądać jak z bajki, wyglądać jak z obrazka, wyglądać jak z żurnala*[12].

Jak pokazuje powyższe zestawienie, wśród polskich frazeologizmów i przysłów nie znajdujemy wyrażeń z nazwami pieniędzy, natomiast w angielszczyźnie występuje stałe połączenie wyrazowe *to look like a million dollars*. Jeśli przetłumaczy się je na język polski i wstawi nazwę polskiej waluty, otrzymane połączenie wyrazowe *wyglądać jak milion złotych* brzmi zaskakująco, a nawet dziwnie – porównywanie atrakcyjnego wyglądu wydaje się nieodpowiednie. Źródła amerykańskiej metafory można upatrywać w głęboko zakorzenionej w protestanckiej religii wierze w ciężką pracę i byciu wynagradzanym za nią, również finansowo. O ile w USA zarabianie i posiadanie pieniędzy są oceniane pozytywnie, o tyle w Polsce, zwłaszcza w okresie socjalizmu, bycie zamożnym było kojarzone z pełnieniem wysokiej funkcji w partii lub z byciem nieuczciwym. Postrzeganie przez Polaków zarabiania pieniędzy zmieniło się po zmianie ustroju, która miała miejsce stosunkowo niedawno, jednak w polszczyźnie omawiana metafora jest nadal nieobecna.

Niezależnie od tego angielskie zapożyczenie *wyglądać jak milion dolarów* zaczęło być używane i zyskuje ono coraz większą popularność. Pojawia się przede wszystkim w tekstach prasowych i internetowych, zwłaszcza w artykułach poświęconych celebrytom, w demotywatorach i wielu innych tekstach. Wyrażenie to stanowi przykład przejętej z języka obcego jednostki, która z jednej strony odzwierciedla zmiany zachodzące w kulturze polskiej, polegające na postrzeganiu wyglądu

---

12 Mirosław Bańko, Słownik porównań, Wydawnictwo Naukowe PWN, Warszawa 2004, s. 189-190.

Moreover, the word dollars connotes America, thus it can be assumed that it triggers positive associations in native users of the Polish language.

To sum up, it can be said that after the statehood transformation of 1989, American culture greatly influenced Poles' way of behaving, which can be attributed to the positive stereotype of the country, being well grounded and fairly stable over a long period of time, and the widespread nature of "Americanness": the elements of American culture in films, television shows, songs and video clips, commercials, advertisements and other texts of culture. Moreover, direct experience, such as working for an American corporation, studying in the USA etc., plays an important role in the incorporation of American culture into the Polish one.

The influences, observed in many areas, manifest themselves clearly in language. They can be determined at various levels: lexical, with many words of Anglo-American origins; phraseological, where fixed word combinations are borrowed; and pragmatic, for instance, dealing with the notion of politeness. What is really important is the fact that the influence does not limit itself to language, but goes much deeper, affecting the culture and value system of the Polish people. In fact, it has an impact on the perception of the world, consequently reflected in words and phrases used for communication. In turn, when such language items are used in discourse, they reinforce the changes in Poles' perceptions of reality.

One can pose a question regarding the evaluation of such changes. Answering it is by no means easy: as already mentioned, over centuries various influences of different cultures have been observed in Polish. Actually, most of them resulted from direct contact, mostly with neighbouring ethnic communities or those

By Dr. Joanna Szerszunowicz

jako ważnego elementu ogólnej oceny, na przykład w trakcie rozmów kwalifikacyjnych, a z drugiej dzięki powszechności użycia wpływa na tworzenie się nowego punktu widzenia.

Omawiane połączenie jest niewątpliwie atrakcyjne z powodu swojej nowości, ale można przyjąć, że jej powodzenie jest również wynikiem tego, że odzwierciedla ona zmiany, które zaszły w percepcji Polaków. Nowe porównania są możliwe, ponieważ zmieniła się rzeczywistość, w której są używane: współczesna kultura po 1989 roku ceni wysoko każdy rodzaj sukcesu, w tym również finansowy. Można przyjąć, że takie podejście wpłynęło na szybką akceptację wyrażenia *to look like a million dollars*. Ponadto warto dodać, że wyraz *dollars* jest kojarzony z Ameryką, zatem całe wyrażenie wywołuje pozytywne odczucia u rodzimych użytkowników języka polskiego.

Wnioski

Podsumowując, można stwierdzić, że po przełomie 1989 roku kultura amerykańska zaczęła znacząco oddziaływać na zachowanie Polaków. Z pewnością duży wpływ na to miały dwa czynniki: pozytywny od wielu lat stereotyp tego kraju i powszechne występowanie elementów kultury amerykańskiej, obecnej w filmach, programach telewizyjnych, piosenkach, wideoklipach, reklamach i innych tekstach kultury. Ponadto bezpośrednie doświadczenia takiej jak praca dla amerykańskiej korporacji, studiowanie w USA itp., odgrywa ważną rolę w oddziaływaniu kultury amerykańskiej na polską.

Wpływy te, widoczne w wielu obszarach, zaznaczają się wyraźnie w języku. Występują one na różnych płaszczyznach: leksykalnej, na której znajdujemy liczne angielskie zapożyczenia, frazeologicznej, gdzie obserwujemy występowanie wyrażeń przejętych z angielszczyzny, i pragmatycznej, na przykład w sferze grzeczności related through political ties with Poland. In the case of America, it is a world-wide impact on many cultures and languages, including Polish. Many linguists express concern regarding the large number of borrowings, and in the same vein, culture specialists comment on the danger of the unification of cultures.

However, it should be remembered that, as Kramsch emphasises, language expresses, embodies and symbolises cultural reality[13]. Therefore, the incorporation of some elements of American culture, connected with the changes occurring in Poland, can be treated as a sign of development, ensuring that the Polish language will express, embody and symbolise the Polish cultural reality in its richness and variety. What is really crucial in this situation is the strength of the Polish sense of cultural identity and their mother tongue awareness, allowing this ethnic community to benefit from foreign influences, among others that of America, turning them into contributions to the Polish language and culture.

13　Claire Kramsch, Language and Culture, Oxford University Press, Oxford 2000, p. 3.

By Dr. Joanna Szerszunowicz

American Influence on Polish Culture
Reflected in Language językowej. Naprawdę ważny jest fakt, że wpływ ten nie ogranicza się do języka, sięga znacznie głębiej, oddziałuje na percepcję świata, co, w konsekwencji, znajduje odzwierciedlenie w słownictwie i wyrażeniach używanych w komunikacji. Z kolei jednostki te stosowane w komunikacji ugruntowują zmiany w postrzeganiu rzeczywistości przez Polaków.

Nasuwa się pytanie dotyczące oceny zmian zachodzących w języku polskim pod wpływem kultury amerykańskiej. Udzielenie na nie odpowiedzi nie jest łatwe: jak już wspomniano, w ciągu stulecia różne kultury oddziaływały na polszczyznę. Jednak większość z tych wpływów wynikała z bezpośrednich kontaktów, głównie ze wspólnotami językowymi sąsiadującymi z Polską lub tych, z którymi łączyły ją relacje polityczne. Ameryka oddziałuje globalnie, na wiele kultur i języków, a polszczyzna jest jednym z nich. Językoznawcy wyrażają zaniepokojenie dotyczące dużej liczby zapożyczeń, wtórują im kulturoznawcy, którzy widzą niebezpieczeństwo w tendencji do unifikacji kultur.

Warto pamiętać, że – jak podkreśla Kramsch – język wyraża, uosabia i symbolizuje rzeczywistość kulturową[13]. Z tego powodu przyswojenie niektórych elementów kultury amerykańskiej, uwarunkowane zmianami w kulturze polskiej, może być traktowane jako przejaw rozwoju, pozwalający polszczyźnie na wyrażanie, uosabianie i symbolizowanie polskiej rzeczywistości kulturowej w całym jej bogactwie i zróżnicowaniu. W tej sytuacji największe znaczenie ma poczucie przynależności kulturowej Polaków i ich świadomość odrębności językowej. To właśnie one umożliwiają tej wspólnocie językowej korzystanie z obcych wpływów, w tym również amerykańskich, w taki sposób, aby ich działanie było korzystne dla polszczyzny i kultury polskiej.

---

13   Claire Kramsch, Language and Culture, Oxford University Press, Oxford 2000, s. 3.

Do Ukrainians Even Exist, or Are They Just 'Little Russians'?

By Elise López

Elise López was born in the Hills where trees were plentiful and skyscrapers scarce. She now lives in the suburbs with her ever-increasing library of books bursting with the knowledge of a thousand authors. During her spare time she conducts research and writes academic pieces for publication. Her areas of interest include Phraseology, Ethno-linguistics, French literature and film, and Soviet and Post-Soviet discourse. She has studied French, Spanish, German, Russian and Polish, and was taught Morse code when she was little.

For many years, I have heard people mutter comments along the lines of "Ukraine? Where the hell is that? Isn't that in Russia?", "They do speak Russian though, don't they?", or "Ukraine, Russia... same diff'". But I have been sensing a change in the air in the last year and a half, as Ukraine is intermittently featured in Australian news headlines thanks to Russia's interest in claiming it piece by piece. Putin's attempts to erase Ukraine from the map -and he has admitted that it happened on his instruction- have merely served to reinforce the existence of the nation by plunging it into headlines across the globe. Now that the truth about Ukraine is finally coming out, people are becoming more aware than ever that Ukraine is its own nation with its own national identity... not to mention its own language.

The idea for this article struck me while once again hearing of the conflict in Ukraine on the news. I had been wondering for some time why it is that Ukraine and Ukrainians seem to pose such an existential threat to Russia and Russians. How can one nation so fervently deny the existence of another, consider that nation's language a mere dialect of its own, its history an invention, and its culture non-existent? Then I heard Putin refer to Ukraine as 'Little Russia'[1]. I had never realised that the title of Tchaikovsky's Second Symphony, Малороссийская, or 'Little Russian', was referring to Ukraine. In my mind, Putin's comments were derogatory towards Ukrainians, but surely not Tchaikovsky's. So naturally, I had to dig a little deeper.

To understand where Ukraine came from we need to delve into the history of Eastern Europe, but there are many different versions of history when it comes to the relationship between Russia and Ukraine, including a great deal of name-calling and frustra-

---

1   Despite the fact that they do not even speak Russian -proven by the fact that he requires a translator when communicating with Ukrainians.

By Elise López

Do Ukrainians Even Exist, or Are They Just
'Little Russians'?

tion. I will not pretend to fully understand the history of Eastern Europe. Being an ardent fence-sitter, I have a tendency to look at a range of accounts and merely observe which facts appear to be the most consistent[2]. However, when it comes to the history of Eastern Europe, the accounts sway back and forth so violently that you start to feel as though you're sailing around Cape Horn in a dinghy. In my attempts to understand whether Ukrainians truly exist or if they are in fact, just 'Little Russians', I found a handful of common facts. The first is an etymological one: in Polish or Russian, *Krai* means 'edge', 'limit' or 'border'. *U* is a preposition meaning 'next to', 'close to' or 'at'. *U kraya* therefore means something along the lines of 'next to the border'. A simple fact. However, to understand this simple fact more fully, we must delve into the past.

In the Beginning...

The truth is, before there were 'Ukrainians' and 'Russians', there was a united medieval state called Kyivan Rus. Founded by the Varangian people from Scandinavia, the new state was made up of the area now occupied by Belarus, Ukraine and Russia[3]. Kyivan Rus was the largest Slavic state and had a capital, located in Kyiv[4]. In the 10th and 11th centuries, this Slavic state flourished, but it was upon the death of Yaroslav the Wise that things went downhill.

Yaroslav the Wise was a great leader. His reign resulted in the codification of law, and he invested in culture and arts. Unfortunately, after his death in the 11th century, tragedy struck Kyivan

---

2   Always taking into account any relevant weaknesses my sources may have, as any good researcher should, of course.

3   -and the many tribes living in this area.

4   -which is now the capital of Ukraine, for those who didn't know.

Rus, when in the style of King Lear, Yaroslav tried to divide up
his empire between his sons. Civil war ensued and the separate
principalities were never fully reunited. This left each of the principalities vulnerable to foreign armies and eventually Kyivan Rus
fell to the Mongolians. The principalities of Kyivan Rus became
tributaries to the 'Golden Horde'. One of these principalities was
called Muscovy; the predecessor of the early modern Tsardom of
Russia. Two others were the principalities of Halych and Volody-
myr-Volynskyi; the predecessors of modern Ukraine.

While King Louis XI was busy unifying France, Ivan the Great was
doing the same in his part of Kyivan Rus. After ending the rule of the
Golden Horde, he expanded the principality of Muscovy to include
several territories formerly held by Kyivan Rus and united them into
a single Russian state. He was thereafter known as Великий князь
всея Руси or 'Grand Prince of all Rus' and the 'gatherer of the Russian lands'. In the meantime, Danylo Romanovych re-united all of
south-western Kyivan Rus, under the name of Principality of Galicia–
Volhynia, or Kingdom of Ruthenia. This included Volhynia, Galicia
and Rus' ancient capital of Kiev. Danylo was crowned 'the first King
of all Rus' by the papal archbishop in Dorohychyn[5]. However, Poland
invaded and took control of a large part of the territory.

The next major development in Ukrainian history, with much
warring with nearby enemies filling in the gaps, was the
development of a Cossack state[6] called the Zaporozhian Host,
which was led by Bohdan Khmelnytsky. The Cossacks were great
fighters. They helped to defend Poland from Turks and Tatars, but
they did not appreciate the cruel enserfment by Polish nobility.
Soon after came 'The Ruin'. The Ruin was a 30-year war between

---

5   In my attempts to remain unbiased, I'm sure you can see my dilemma.

6   Although the state was not so official, it was a military state with good fighters, so the Polish nobility could hardly argue with those involved.

By Elise López

Do Ukrainians Even Exist, or Are They Just
'Little Russians'?

Russia, Poland, the Turks and the Cossacks over the territory of Ukraine. Khmelnytsky was deserted by his Tatar allies and turned to the Russian Tsar for help. After signing the Treaty of Pereyaslav, the Cossacks had sworn their loyalty to the Russian Tsar. The wars devastated the nations with hundreds of thousands of deaths and the Cossack defeat resulted in the Ukrainian lands being divided up between the victors: Poland and Russia[7].

A new region formed, called New Russia, which was settled by Ukrainians and Russians. However, the Ukrainian elite and the Cossacks never received the freedoms and the autonomy that were promised in the Treaty of Pereyaslav. Within the Empire, it was possible for Ukrainians to rise to the highest ranks of Russian state and church offices, but later, tsarists established a policy of russification, banning the use of the Ukrainian language in public, and in print. This was the beginning of the 'Little Russians'.

Who are the 'Little Russians'?

The term 'Little Russia' is a historical one, used in the 19th century, when Ukraine was seen as part of the triune Russian nation, which consisted of Greater Russia, White Russia and Lower Russia. The term was widely used and was not considered derogatory. When asked about the popular use of the term 'Little Russia', one Ukrainian man[8] said "my dear father was born on their fine dacha in the Ukraine. As a boy he joined the heroic Russian White Army 1917-1921, and he fought the vile Bolsheviks. Their dacha was in Poltava where Peter the Great defeated the combined armies of the brilliant King Karl XII of Sweden and the Cossack warlord Ivan Mazepa. My father and my uncle called Poltava *'MALORossia'*."

---

7   At this point we can begin to see where the name U Kraya came from.

8   -who shall remain anonymous for his own protection during this heated debate

The term 'Little Russian', referring to the Ukrainian people, is a little more complicated. Tchaikovsky's Second Symphony is called 'Little Russian', because it contains Ukrainian folk music. Tchaikovsky's intentions were not derogatory towards Ukrainians, as far as I am aware. He was referring to the language or its people in geographical terms, which was acceptable at that time. In fact, a lot of Ukrainians identified themselves as 'Little Russian' at the time; as 'Little Russian' people, who speak their 'Little Russian' language. But during the 20th century, when Ukraine began to redefine its culture as distinctly Ukrainian, this became less acceptable.

After the Russian Revolution, Ukraine underwent a linguistic and cultural revival in what was remembered as something of a renaissance, encouraged by the communist leader, Mykola Skrypnyk. This began to reverse the damage caused by the Tsardom's russification policies... at least until the 1930s when Stalin came to power. Stalin's policies meant that Russian was spoken in schools, Ukrainians could not practice their religion[9], and even the colourful Ukrainian embroidered shirts had to be covered. Ukrainians had no freedom to express their identity. After Stalin wiped out approximately a quarter of the rural population with his man-made famine[10], those who were still alive and in Ukraine were forced into collectivised farms. This turned the 'bread-basket' of Europe into a wasteland of despair.

After spending most of the century under the repressive Soviet regime and more than three centuries under de facto Russian rule, Ukraine finally declared its independence in 1991.

---

9   In fact, priests were rounded up and executed.

10   The actual number varies greatly between reports. The Soviets were never fond of record-keeping. However, first-hand accounts of the famine have described whole villages being wiped out.

Do Ukrainians Even Exist, or Are They Just 'Little Russians'?

By Elise López

"We are Ukrainians!"
Ukrainian identity in the twenty-first century

Fifteen years into the 21st century, Ukraine is now an established nation. Yet for some reason, Russia cannot let go. In an interview with French television journalist Jean-Pierre Elkabbach in 2012, the Russian Ambassador to France, Alexander Orlov, said "Russians and Ukrainians are one nation. It's like the Bretons and the Normans in France. You can't separate them." He may think that Russia and Ukraine are one nation, but Ukrainians most certainly do not. Putin's thoughts on the matter are clear: "Ukraine is not even a state!" He reportedly told U.S. President George W. Bush during the 2008 NATO summit in Bucharest[11]. His new wave of attempted russification started with the illegal annexation of Crimea in March 2014. Overnight, Ukrainians reported that "little green men" appeared and started a rebellion. These "little green men" were not aliens, but Russian militants with the insignia removed from their uniforms. Putin admitted this only after his plans to annex Crimea were successful enough to make the world question whether the territory is now independent or not.

His next target involves the Eastern regions, where the death toll is increasing on a regular basis. What many Russians apparently refuse to believe is that Ukraine is a separate nation. Instead, Ukraine is seen as a little brother, whom ought to be reunited with his older sibling, but nations do not unify unless both parties agree. In this case, Ukrainians see themselves as a separate nation with a separate identity and the history of Ukraine clearly supports this idea, so they have no reason to unify with Russia. They have a history, language and culture of their own, so it wouldn't make sense to throw it all away, just to be united under Russian hegemony.

---

11   Clearly he is ill-informed of Ukrainian history, unlike you dear readers.

The people of Ukraine only ask for the right to an identity of their own and the acknowledgement of a nation that has as much right to exist as Russia itself. Only then can they truly be free 'Ukrainians' and finally put the term 'Little Russians' to rest. Unfortunately, history has a way of repeating itself. There is a distinct connection between the atrocities of the past and those unfolding before our eyes. It makes me wonder how the cycle will end. The people of Ukraine are standing up and saying "We are Ukrainians!", but will their voices be heard or will they once again be relegated to the status of 'Little Russians'?

By Elise López

Do Ukrainians Even Exist, or Are They Just
'Little Russians'?

<u>References</u>

Bohm, M. 2013. 'Ukraine Is Putin's Favorite Vassal,' The Moscow Times. Available at http://www.themoscowtimes.com/opinion/article/ukraine-is-putins-favorite-vassal/492096.html. Accessed 2 April 2015.

Mykhailo Zhdan. 1988. In Volodymyr Kubijovyc (ed.) Encyclopedia of Ukraine, vol. 2. Toronto: University of Toronto Press.

Pelenski, J. 1998. The Contest for the Legacy of Kievan Rus'. Colorado: East European Monographs.

Remy, J. 2007. 'The Valuev Circular and Censorship of Ukrainian Publications in the Russian Empire (1863–1876): Intention and Practice,' Canadian Slavonic Papers 47: 87–110.

Skinner, B. 2005. 'Borderlands of Faith: Reconsidering the Origins of a Ukrainian Tragedy,' Slavic Review 64(1): 88–116.

Romeo and Snow White

Romeo and Snow White

by Alfindy Agyputri

Alfindy Agyputri, an eighteen year-old student in her second year at Curtin University who is studying Creative Writing and Screen Arts, has always loved writing, reading, and watching movies. She doesn't think writing is just about being published, but more about being read. She writes everything she wants to write, anywhere, anytime, for anyone.

I walked down the hospital corridor with wide paces, smiling and saying a simple "hi" to the nurses and fellow doctors I passed by.

"Going somewhere, Doc?" asked Marni, a nurse who only joined the hospital a few months ago. "Aren't you joining us for the roof-top New Year's party?"

I shook my head with a thin smile, but before I could give any response, another nurse interrupted.

"Doctor Ethan's got something better to do," Susi commented as she smiled knowingly at me, which I responded to by rolling my eyes.

"You guys have fun." I waved at them and several other nurses and doctors who were heading to the elevator with the same knowing smiles.

I rolled my eyes at them because I could guess what was running through their heads at that moment. Every New Year's Eve, all the doctors, nurses, and staff in the hospital would gather on the roof to celebrate together. They would have a small BBQ party as they counted down to the New Year together and watched the fireworks held by the hotel across the street.

I used to turn up to the party every year, but for the past two years – ever since a particular girl was admitted here, to be exact – I had another small party to celebrate on New Year's Eve.

Many would say (especially those young nurses who liked to gossip. And they thought I didn't know what they'd been saying about me behind my back) I'd supposedly fallen in love with this girl. Yeah, right! I was heading into my 30s now, while that girl had

by Alfindy Agyputri

Romeo
and Snow White

Aku melangkah lebar-lebar menyusuri lorong rumah sakit sambil sesekali tersenyum dan menyapa suster-suster maupun sesama dokter yang berpapasan denganku.

"Mau kemana, Dok?" tanya Marni, suster yang baru beberapa bulan ini bergabung di rumah sakit. "Tidak ikut ke pesta tahun baru di atap?"

Aku menggeleng sambil tersenyum tipis, tetapi belum sempat aku menjawab, suster lainnya memotong.

"Dokter Ethan mah punya acara lain," komentar Susi sambil tersenyum penuh arti ke arahku, yang kutanggapi dengan memutar bola mataku.

"Kalian selamat bersenang-senang, ya." Aku melambai ke arah segerembolan suster dan dokter yang sedang bergerak ke arah lift dengan senyuman penuh arti yang sama.

Aku kembali memutar bola mata karena bisa menebak apa yang sedang mereka pikirkan saat itu. Setiap malam tahun baru, para dokter, suster, dan karyawan lain yang bekerja di rumah sakit akan berkumpul di atap gedung untuk merayakan bersama. Ada pesta BBQ kecil-kecilan sambal menanti detik-detik menuju tahun baru bersama-sama dan menonton pesta kembang api yang diadakan oleh gedung hotel di seberang jalan.

Aku selalu hadir di pesta ini setiap tahun, tetapi dua tahun belakangan ini – tepatnya sejak gadis itu mulai dirawat di sini – aku jadi punya pesta kecil-kecilan lain untuk merayakan malam tahun baru.

Romeo
and Snow White

only turned 17. I always treated her as if she was my own little sister, but I knew that this reason wasn't good enough for those gossip-loving nurses.

My feet stopped right in front of a white door with number 77 on it. I knocked on the door twice, and spun the handle without waiting for any response. Once the door swung open, my eyes immediately caught an unusual sight.

The same girl was still lying down on the hospital bed in her favourite green pajamas, staring straight ahead blankly. But her slender eyes no longer sparkled, and her pale face showed no sign of a smile, not even a fake one.

I cleared my throat as I lifted three boxes of DVDs in my right hand. "Look what I've got. Your favourite movies."

There was one compulsory movie that we had to watch every New Year's Eve - *New Year's Eve*. Then the rest were just any movies on her to-watch list. Most of them were romantic-comedies or sad romantic movies that would make you cry. For this time, I chose *Just My Luck* and *Chasing Liberty*. Yeah, call me a freak for choosing to watch chick flicks, but at least it was better than *P.S I Love You* or *The Notebook*. I was not in the mood to watch cheesy romantic-tragedies.

The girl turned her head a little towards me, still without smiling, then turned her souless eys back to the big window next to her bed. There was nothing to see, really. There were only old buildings lined up with messy landscape all around. Our location was a little odd. There was a big busy street in front of the hospital, along with tall buildings, but at the back, there was nothing worth looking at.

by Alfindy Agyputri

Romeo
and Snow White

Banyak yang bilang (terutama para suster muda yang suka menggosip itu. Dan mereka kira aku tidak tahu apa yang mereka omongkan tentangku di belakangku) aku telah jatuh cinta pada gadis ini. Yang benar saja! Aku sudah hampir berkepala tiga, sedangkan gadis itu baru berumur tujuh belas tahun. Aku selalu menganggapnya seperti adikku sendiri, tapi aku tahu alasan itu tidak cukup bagus untuk para suster penggosip itu.

Langkahku berhenti tepat di depan pintu putih dengan nomor 77 yang terpampang di atasnya. Aku mengetuk pintu itu dua kali, lalu memutar gagangnya tanpa menunggu sahutan. Begitu pintu terbuka, mataku langsung menangkap pemandangan yang tidak lazim.

Gadis yang sama masih terbaring di atas ranjang rumah sakit dalam balutan piyama hijau favoritnya, menatap lurus ke depan dengan hampa. Tapi mata sipitnya tak lagi bersinar, dan tak ada bekas senyuman di wajah pucatnya, bahkan senyuman palsu sekalipun.

Aku berdeham sambil mengacungkan tiga buah kotak DVD di tangan kananku. "Lihat apa yang kubawa. Film-film favoritmu."

Film yang wajib kami nonton setiap malam tahun baru adalah *New Year's Eve*. Sisanya adalah film apa saja yang termasuk dalam to-watch list milik gadis ini. Biasanya sih film romantis-komedi atau film romantis yang bikin nangis. Pilihanku untuk hari ini adalah *Just My Luck* dan *Chasing Liberty*. Yeah, call me a freak karena memilih untuk menonton chick flicks seperti itu, tapi ini lebih baik daripada *P.S I Love You* atau *The Notebook*. Aku sedang tidak berminat menonton film-film romantis tragis yang cheesy.

Romeo
and Snow White

This was what was unusual. This girl might not be the most cheerful person in the world, but she always managed a smile, no matter how thin and how fake it was to me. But today, nothing.

I walked towards her bed. "Hey, what's the matter?"

The Singaporean girl could speak Indonesian well, since her mom was also Indonesian, but sometimes, or most of the time, we just spoke English. She didn't respond, only embraced her legs even tighter.

I sat next to her to push her chin up until our eyes met. "Madz, what's wrong?"

Madz looked at me with her black eyes. "Do you love me?" she asked out of the blue.

I cleared my throat. "Of course," I said in a low tone, then quick-ly added, "As a friend, or a sister, or anything you want to be." I almost slapped my own forehead. What kind of answer was that?

Thankfully, Madz didn't seem to mind. She continued, "It's been two years now, or even more, but nothing changes. It'll be a new year tomorrow, again, and I'm sure I'll always be the same sick girl who will rot to death here."

I gulped. There were times when Madz started to whine, making no sense, and they were my least favourite moments. She would complain about her condition that never seemed to show any progress, then she would start to make ridiculous wishes.

by Alfindy Agyputri

Romeo
and Snow White

Gadis itu menoleh sedikit ke arahku, masih tanpa senyum, lalu kembali menatap hampa ke arah jendela besar di samping tempat tidurnya. Tidak ada apa-apa yang bisa dinikmati dari pemandangan di baliknya. Hanya ada gedung-gedung ruko yang berhimpitan di sekitar gedung rumah sakit. Lokasi kami memang sedikit aneh. Di depan gedung ini ada jalan raya lebar dan gedung-gedung tinggi yang cukup megah, tetapi di bagian belakang, tidak ada yang bisa dipandangi.

Inilah yang tidak lazim. Gadis ini memang bukan gadis paling ceria sedunia, tapi ia selalu melemparkan senyum, setipis dan sepalsu apapun itu padaku. Tapi hari ini, nihil.

Aku berjalan menghampiri ranjangnya. "Hey, what's the matter?"

Gadis keturunan Singapura ini memang bisa berbahasa Indonesia dengan lancar, mengingat ibunya yang juga orang Indonesia, tapi terkadang, atau seringnya, kami mengobrol dalam bahasa Inggris.

Gadis itu tidak merespon. Ia hanya mempererat pelukan pada kedua lututnya.

Aku duduk di sebelahnya dan mengangkat dagunya untuk menatapku. "Madz, what's wrong?"

Madz menatapku dengan kedua mata hitamnya. "Do you love me?" tanyanya tiba-tiba.

Aku berdeham. "Tentu saja," sahutku pelan, lalu buru-buru melanjutkan. "Sebagai teman, atau adik, or anything you want to be." Ingin rasanya aku menepuk dahiku sendiri. Jawaban macam apa itu?

Romeo
and Snow White

"Suicide or euthanasia is not a solution," I said in a firm, final tone. She often asked me to stop her treatment – medication and chemotherapy. She even asked me to give her cyanide one time, to hasten the process.

"I'll die anyway. Rather than being a burden to Dad, it's better to use the money for something more useful, like opening a new business and funding Kyle and Nigel's schooling."

Madz was the firstborn from a couple made up of a Singaporean man and an Indonesian woman who came from Palembang. They used to live in Singapore, but ever since Madz was diagnosed, they all moved to Batam, a small town close to Singapore – about 45 minutes by ferry – because her parents couldn't fund her treatment in Singapore. One year after the move, Madz's mom died of a heart attack.

Madz always thought of herself as a burden to her family. Her dad had to work at several places to pay for her treatment and her little brothers' education, and Kyle and Nigel, who were still very young, almost dropped out of school to help make ends meet. At that point, I secretly helped them out, and offered more help for Madz's treatment, but Madz found out and refused it firmly. Ever since then, her death wish became more frequent.

"The cancer is spreading, and it'll only get worse, with or without these stupid medical treatments. You're only wasting your time, energy, and money. I don't want you to regret it when you see me in a graveyard instead of this hospital bed."

I hated to admit it, but she was such a selfish girl. She didn't think of the consequences of her death wish. Firstly, I would be charged for her murder, for practicing euthanasia illegally –

by Alfindy Agyputri

Romeo
and Snow White

Untungnya, Madz tidak tampak keberatan. Ia meneruskan, "Sudah dua tahun aku di sini, bahkan lebih, tapi tak ada yang berubah. Besok sudah tahun baru lagi, dan aku yakin aku akan tetap menjadi gadis penyakitan yang akan mati membusuk di sini."

Aku meneguk ludah. Ada saat-saat tertentu ketika Madz mulai mengeluh dan melantur, dan itu adalah saat-saat yang paling kubenci. Ia akan mengeluh tentang kondisinya yang tidak pernah menunjukkan progres, dan mulai memohon yang aneh-aneh padaku.

"Bunuh diri atau eutanasia bukanlah solusi," sahutku tegas. Ia sering memohon agar aku menghentikan perawatannya – pengobatan dan kemoterapi. Ia bahkan pernah memintaku untuk memberinya sianida untuk mempercepat prosesnya.

"Toh aku akan mati juga nantinya. Daripada menjadi beban untuk Ayah, lebih baik uangnya dipakai untuk sesuatu yang lebih berguna, seperti membuka usaha baru dan membiayai sekolah Kyle dan Nigel."

Madz adalah anak sulung dari pasangan pria Singapura dan wanita Palembang. Mereka tadinya tinggal di Singapura, tapi sejak Madz divonis, mereka semua pindah ke Batam, sebuah kota kecil dekat Singapura – hanya berjarak 45 menit naik ferry – karena kedua orangtuanya tidak sanggup membiayai perawatannya di Singapura. Setahun setelah kepindahan mereka, ibu Madz meninggal karena serangan jantung.

Madz selalu menganggap dirinya beban bagi keluarganya. Ayahnya harus bekerja di banyak tempat untuk membiayai perawatan Madz dan juga sekolah kedua adiknya.Lalu Kyle dan Nigel

I didn't know how many years of imprisonment I'd get for that. Once I'd tried to discuss this matter with her.

"I don't want to be a murderer," I said to her that time.

And guess what she said? "Take it as a mercy killing. That's what people call it. It's for the best."

She always said that – "It's for the best". Frankly, I didn't even care if I was arrested for her wish. It used to be my main argument not to grant her wish. But then, as I got to know her better, all I thought of was how sad we would feel, the people she would leave behind. That was what made her selfish. She didn't think of the people who would be left behind.

Even though she saw herself as a burden, I knew that her dad and brothers really loved her. Her dad worked really hard for her, and her brothers never forgot to visit their sister in hospital. I could see in her eyes how happy she was every time her family came to visit. They were the only ones who could put a wide smile on her face, or even make her laugh. I knew for sure she didn't want to leave them.

"It's not that I don't want to stay with you guys anymore, but this is the best for all of us. We are all going to be free. You and the hospital will be free from the troubles that I cause. Dad will be free from debts and his pile of work. My little brothers will be free from money problems for their education. And I'll be free from this pain."

I hate it when she's right. I didn't mind at all to take care of her, to keep treating her, and the financial problems weren't a big deal either, because I could still help them out with it. But every time

by Alfindy Agyputri

Romeo
and Snow White

yang masih kecil-kecil sempat terancam putus sekolah karena kekurangan biaya. Saat itu, aku memutuskan untuk membantu mereka diam-diam, dan juga menawarkan bantuan untuk biaya perawatan Madz, tapi tertangkap basah oleh Madz yang langsung menolak mentah-mentah. Death wish miliknya itu pun menjadi semakin sering disebut.

"Kankerku menyebar, dan akan terus memburuk, dengan atau tanpa pengobatan bodoh ini. Kalian hanya membuang waktu, tenaga, dan uang saja. Aku tidak mau kalian menyesal saat melihat aku yang akhirnya terbaring di liang kubur, bukan di ranjang rumah sakit lagi."

Aku benci mengakuinya, tapi Madz itu sangat egois. Ia tidak memikirkan akibat dari permohonannya itu. Pertama, aku akan dituduh sebagai pembunuhnya karena melakukan tindakan eutanasia yang jelas terlarang – aku tidak tahu berapa tahun aku akan dipenjara. Aku pernah mencoba mendiskusikan hal ini padanya.

"Aku tidak mau menjadi seorang pembunuh," ucapku saat itu.

Dan tebak apa yang dikatakannya? "Anggap saja ini mercy killing. That's what people call it. Ini kan, untuk kebaikan kita semua."

Selalu itu yang dikatakannya – "Ini untuk kebaikan kita semua". Jujur saja, aku tidak benar-benar peduli kalau aku masuk penjara karena permintaannya. Awalnya memang itu alasan utamaku untuk tidak mengabulkan permintaannya. Tapi, setelah lama mengenalnya, yang kupikirkan adalah seberapa sedih kami yang akan ditinggalkannya nanti. Itulah yang membuatnya egois. Ia tidak memikirkan orang-orang yang ditinggalkannya.

I was reminded of the pain she had to go through, either from the cancer or the chemotherapy, I lost my stance.

I glanced at the door, then at the DVDs that I had brought. Watching movies didn't always help. It didn't always entertain us or help us to escape the reality. I decided to put the DVDs away. Change of plan.

"Wait here," I said and I left the room.

Voices in my mind, from both the angel and the devil, haunted me all the way, but both reached one conclusion – one thing that felt right. I entered the kitchen and grabbed a red apple, Madz's favourite, from the refrigerator, then stopped by at the dispensary next door to collect one last item on my way back to Madz's room. When I returned, Madz was staring at me with curious eyes.

"What's your New Year's resolution for this coming year?" I asked. The same question I always asked on a New Year's Eve.

Madz put on a straight face. "It's the same as any other year."

I nodded. "Well, your wish is my command," I almost whispered as I handed her the red apple.

Madz received it in wonder, but then she put her straight face back on. "Even my favourite red apple won't do much this time," she said, but still took one bite.

She usually felt a little better after eating, and I'd always been sure that it was what she needed the most, including now, even though she said it wouldn't work.

by Alfindy Agyputri

**Romeo
and Snow White**

Walaupun ia menganggap dirinya beban, aku tahu ayah dan kedua adiknya sangat menyayanginya. Ayahnya bekerja sangat keras demi dirinya, dan kedua adiknya selalu rajin menjenguk kakak mereka di rumah sakit. Aku juga bisa melihat seberapa senangnya Madz setiap kali keluarganya datang menjenguk. Hanya mereka yang bisa membuatnya tersenyum lebar atau tertawa terbahak-bahak. Aku yakin ia pun tidak mau meninggalkan mereka.

"Bukannya aku tidak mau bersama kalian lagi, tapi ini untuk kebaikan kita semua. Kita akan terbebas. Kau dan rumah sakit akan terbebas dari kerepotan mengurusiku. Ayah akan terbebas dari jerat hutang dan pekerjaannya yang menggunung. Adik-adikku akan terbebas dari masalah ekonomi untuk sekolah mereka. Dan aku akan terbebas dari rasa sakit ini."

Aku benci saat Madz memaparkan kenyataan. Aku sama sekali tidak keberatan mengurusinya, dan masalah ekonomi pun bukan masalah besar, karena aku masih bisa membantu mereka. Tapi, setiap kali aku mengingat rasa sakit yang harus dirasakan Madz, baik dari penyakit maupun dari proses kemoterapinya, pertahananku melemah.

Aku melirik pintu, lalu kotak-kotak DVD yang kubawa. Menonton film tidak selalu menghibur dan membantu kami lari kenyataan. Aku pun meletakkan kotak-kotak DVD itu di atas meja. Perubahan rencana.

"Tunggu di sini," ucapku lalu meninggalkan ruangan.

Berbagai suara, baik dari si malaikat maupun setan, menghantuiku sepanjang perjalanan, namun keduanya sampai pada satu kesimpulan – sesuatu yang terasa sangat tepat untuk dilakukan.

Well, Madz had never been a super-optimistic girl. But I knew, once upon a time, she had the will and faith to recover, but along the way, she started to lose it. And I watched as her faith faded. This was the risk that came with being a doctor. I was reminded of one suggestion a senior doctor once gave me. "It's best not to get attached to your patients, because it's just easier for you to let them go when the time comes."

He was right. I knew it well, because it happened to my first patient, a ten year-old boy with bone cancer. He was so optimistic that he would recover. This genius boy always got first place in his classes at school. I really loved him as my own little brother. And like my senior said, when this patient had to leave, my heart was scattered to pieces. From then on, I didn't really bother to get attached to anyone, until I met her.

I began to hear a struggling noise coming from Madz. After swallowing her first bite of the apple, her forehead creased and her hands were gripping her chest. She struggled to catch a breath, making weird noises from her throat. She stared at me with an undefined look. I could only stare back at her without giving any other response.

My hands started to grip on the cylinder I was holding. Now Madz looked exactly like Snow White – that was what I always called her, because her hair was as black as night and her skin was as white as snow. But her lips were no longer as red as blood. They too were as pale as snow. Well, now we can say she looked more like Sleeping Beauty. Both of her eyes were closed with a peaceful smile on her face. I guess I managed to grant her wish – her last wish as well as her New Year's resolution. For us to be free.

by Alfindy Agyputri

Romeo
and Snow White

Aku memasuki dapur dan mengambil sebutir apel merah, buah kesukaan Madz, dari dalam kulkas, lalu mampir ke rumah obat di sebelahnya untuk mengambil satu benda terakhir dalam perjalanan menuju kamar Madz. Saat aku kembali, Madz menatapku penuh tanda tanya.

"Apa resolusimu untuk tahun depan?" tanyaku. Pertanyaan sama yang selalu kutanyakan setiap malam tahun baru.

Madz memasang ekspresi datar. "Sama seperti tahun-tahun sebelumnya."

Aku mengangguk. "Well, your wish is my command," sahutku pelan sambil mengulurkan sebutir apel merah.

Walaupun heran, Madz tetap menerimanya. "Apel merah favoritku pun tidak akan mempan kali ini," ujarnya, tapi ia tetap menggigit apel itu.

Madz biasanya merasa sedikit lebih baik setelah makan, dan aku cukup yakin itulah yang paling ia butuhkan, walaupun ia mengatakan kali ini tidak akan mempan.

Well, Madz memang bukan tipe gadis yang super-optimistic. Tapi aku tahu, dulu, ia punya keinginan dan keyakinan untuk sembuh, namunlama kelamaan, ia kehilangan keyakinan. Dan aku menyaksikan kelunturan rasa percayanya. Inilah risiko menjadi seorang dokter. Aku jadi ingat saran dari salah satu dokter senior. "Lebih baik tidak terikat perasaan dengan pasienmu, karena akan lebih sulit untuk melepas mereka kalau sudah sampai pada waktunya."

I closed my eyes as I clutched the cylinder in my right hand tighter.

They are right when they say, "When you're about to die, your life flashes before your eyes." I remembered the first time that girl became our patient. At first, she disliked Batam, an environment that was too different from Singapore. But one thing that had never been a problem for Madz, the food. She fell in love with Indonesian cuisine straight away. I often became the delivery service to buy her whatever food she wanted to taste.

In the two years we'd been together, we had established a routine which filled up the hours between my work with other patients. It was a full time job in itself, but I treasured every moment.

I glanced at the girl who lay peacefully on the hospital bed. I wonder what flashed before her eyes. My right hand was gripping the cylinder tighter. I closed my eyes again and took a long deep breath before stabbing my own neck with the sharp end of the cylinder – right in the artery.

I was struggling to reach for Madz's hand which had already lost its warmth. I managed a thin smile, knowing what would come. "See you soon, Madz."

The cylinder slipped through my fingers and I watched as the carefully labelled "cyanide" cylinder rolled across the floor.

I heard faint noises from outside the window, people shouting simultaneously, along with other noises from the trumpets and fireworks. "Three... Two... One!"

by Alfindy Agyputri

**Romeo
and Snow White**

Beliau benar. Aku tahu betul, karena itu terjadi pada pasien pertamaku, anak laki-laki berumur sepuluh yang menderita kanker tulang. Ia begitu optimis akan kesembuhannya. Anak jenius itu selalu meraih ranking satu di sekolahnya. Aku menyayanginya seperti adikku sendiri. Dan seperti yang dikatakan seniorku, ketika akhirnya ia meninggal dunia, hatiku benar-benar hancur. Sejak itu, aku tidak mau terikat lagi pada siapapun, sampai aku bertemu dengan gadis itu.

Aku mendengar suara desahan aneh yang berasal dari Madz. Baru saja ia mengunyah dan menelan satu gigit apel merah itu, dahinya berkerut dan tangannya mencengkeram dada. Suara nafasnya mulai terdengar aneh karena kesulitan bernafas. Ia menatapku dengan tatapan yang tak terdefinisikan, sedangkan aku hanya bisa menatapnya balik tanpa memberikan respon apapun.

Tanganku ikut mencengkeram silinder yang berada di dalam genggaman. Sekarang Madz sudah benar-benar tampak seperti Snow White – aku selalu menganggapnya seperti si putri salju, karena rambutnya yang sehitam malam dan kulitnya yang seputih salju. Tetapi bibirnya tak lagi semerah darah. Bibirnya pun ikut sepucat salju sekarang. Well, bisa dibilang ia lebih mirip Sleeping Beauty sekarang. Kedua matanya tertutup dengan senyuman damai menghiasi wajahnya. Kurasa aku berhasil mengabulkan permintaannya – permintaan terakhir sekaligus resolusi tahun barunya. For us to be free.

Aku memejamkan kedua mataku sambil menggenggam silinder di tangan kananku lebih erat. Sekarang giliranku untuk menjadi Romeo untuk Snow White-ku.

Mereka benar saat mereka bilang, "When you're about to die, your life flashes before your eyes." Aku ingat saat gadis itu pertama

Romeo
and Snow White

by Alfindy Agyputri

kali menjadi pasien kami. Awalnya, ia tidak begitu menyukai Batam, dengan suasana yang sangat berbeda dari Singapura. Tapi, satu hal yang tidak pernah menjadi masalah bagi Madz, makanannya. Ia langsung jatuh cinta pada makanan khas Indonesia. Aku sering menjadi kurir makanan untuk gadis itu, membelikan makanan apa saja yang ia inginkan.

Selama dua tahun kami bersama, kami memiliki rutinitas tersendiri yang mengisi jam-jam kerjaku dengan pasien lagi. Itu menjadikan pekerjaan ini full time, tapi aku menikmati setiap detiknya.

Aku melirik gadis yang terbaring damai di atas ranjang rumah sakit. Aku penasaran apa yang terlintas di benaknya sebelum semuanya berakhir. Cengkeraman tangan kananku semakin erat. Aku memejamkan kedua mataku dan menarik nafas dalam-dalam sebelum menancapkan ujung runcing dari silinder yang kugenggam tepat di urat nadi leherku.

Dengan susah payah, aku meraih tangan kanan Madz yang sudah kehilangan kehangatannya dan tersenyum kecil, karena aku sudah tahu apa yang akan terjadi. "See you soon, Madz."

Silinder tersebut terlepas dari genggaman jari-jariku dan aku menyaksikan silinder yang dilabeli "sianida" dengan hati-hati itu berguling di lantai.

Sayup-sayup terdengar riuh-rendah dari luar jendela, teriakan-teriakan kompak orang-orang, diiringi suara-suara berisik lainnya dari terumpet dan kembang api. "Tiga... Dua... Satu!"

EVA KANTŮRKOVÁ
TAJEMSTVÍ SAMETU
@
O zákulisí převratu 1989
s režisérem JIŘÍM SVOBODOU
FINDER
ANGLICKO
ČESKY
PRAKTICKÝ ČESKO
ANGLICKY
slovník
nové vydání
Marta Šrámková
POD
BRNĚNSKÝMI
VĚŽEMI
DOPLNĚK

Learning Czech Through Literature

By Raelke Grimmer

Raelke is a writer and linguist and the Founding Editor of Tongues. She is a PhD candidate in Creative Writing at Flinders University, researching the genre of language journalism and writing a book about monolingualism and multiculturalism in Australia.

I am both a bibliophile (a person who loves reading and collecting books) and a linguaphile (a person who loves languages). My bibliophilism emerged first, before I could even read for myself. Our house was full of books, and the library wasn't far away, so every couple of weeks I got to choose some new worlds to take home with me. When I began school, I learnt to read and never stopped. I asked for books for birthday and Christmas presents, and when I finally got my first job I spent my first hard-earned dollars on books. But not just on any books: on books about language and linguistics.

My interest in language didn't develop until I started high school, despite the eight years of Japanese lessons I toiled through in primary school. These classes were culture lessons under the guise of language lessons. Eight years later I could fold origami like a pro, tell a dramatic rendition of the story of Sadako and sumo wrestle with the best of them (well, push my opponents safely out of a circle). I could name a few animals, a few colours, speak my name and count to ninety-nine, and only ninety-nine, because I always forgot the Japanese word for one hundred.

My linguaphilism began to take shape as I started German lessons in high school which, after my primary school experiences, were full-on, intense language lessons. Sure, the teachers still spoke English more often than not, and we spent heaps of lessons learning about German history, but I was discovering names for grammatical constructions I didn't even know existed before. I fell in love with German immediately, but I wasn't content to stop there. As soon as I was able to, in Year 11, I added Spanish as another language. At the end of that year, I went on an exchange trip to Germany for two and a half months, and my language learning bubble came crashing down.

By Raelke Grimmer

Learning Czech
Through Literature

The German language completely baffled me for the first week I was in the country, but my host parents couldn't speak English, so I was forced into using German. At the school I went to, the coordinator of the exchange program put up a flyer about us exchange students, along with our photo. The photo was accompanied by text which introduced us to any student who cared to read the sign, and ex-plained that our German was terrible but we were learning, so don't be afraid to talk to us. As Year 11 students we were then placed in classes with Year 5 and 6 students instead of with our peers, in the hope we would understand more of the lessons. In fact, it had the opposite affect and made us feel even more out of place. The students in my Year 6 class had one year of English lessons behind them, yet they could communicate with me in English much better than I could communicate with them after four years of German lessons. And I wasn't even a bad student. I attended the English classes with students my age, and the entire class was conducted in English. If a student got told off, they got told off in English. If they had questions about the assignments, they asked for clarification in English. They even watched Al Gore's *An Inconvenient Truth-* in English, without subtitles. Back home in our German class, *An Inconvenient Truth* would have been *Kommissar Rex* (*Inspector Rex*) and there would have been bright yellow English subtitles to ensure we understood. By the end of the two and a half month exchange, my German had improved to the point where I was almost fluent. I had one of the best times of my life in the Hugendubel bookstore in the centre of Munich, and packed my suitcase with German, Span-ish and French books to take with me back home.

Far from curing me of my linguaphilism, this experience only spurred me on and made me more determined than ever to learn languages, and learn them well. When I started university, German wasn't offered so I decided to try French for a year. Our lessons were separated out into grammar lessons and conversation tutorials. We were given tests every two weeks, which I aced because I have a good memory and I could memorise the rules and vocabulary they were testing us on. We weren't given a formal oral assessment until the second semester, which I just about failed. My French accent emerged as a Spanish accent. After one year, I left French behind.

All my experiences with language learning were essentially the same. We would read conversations in the target language in class, and then reproduce some of our own. We would learn grammar rules and do repetitive exercises aimed to drill the rules into our brains, and we would learn about the culture and history of the countries, with English used as the language of instruction for those lessons. I never took history as a subject in high school, so at least my language lessons covered that. But there had to be a better way to learn a language. A way that made more sense, and that equipped me with the skills to actually use the language in a meaningful way when the need arose.

During my Masters in Applied Linguistics, I was introduced to text-based language teaching, a method based on linguist MAK Halliday's theory of Systemic Functional Grammar. The theory behind the approach is that before a student enters a language learning classroom, they already have a lot of experience with language and a lot of experience with texts. In order to successfully learn a foreign language, the language needs to be taught in context for a social purpose, and not in isolated grammatical and lexical units. The texts should be authentic, and convey meaning. A text can be written or spoken and any length.

As a bibliophile and linguaphile, this approach immediately made sense to me. I always sought out articles, TV programs and books to read in the languages I was learning, to see if I could put what

By Raelke Grimmer

Learning Czech
Through Literature

I knew into practice. For the most part, we weren't given these resources in class, so I would hunt them down for myself. This approach also seemed to favour fluency over accuracy, where communicating an idea is considered to be more important than nit-picking perfect grammar. Grammar is essential in being able to communicate, but there comes a point where even if the learner's grammar is not at the stage of perfection, they can be understood.

I had two questions about this approach, both of which fed into my bibliophilism and linguaphilism: would it work for the self-learner and would it work using literature texts? To complete my Masters, I had to write an 18,000 word dissertation based on original research. To investigate my questions, I decided to teach myself Czech by reading books written in Czech.

Why Czech? The text-based approach emphasises that the learner needs to have a social purpose for learning the language. The learner needs to know why they are learning the language and what they hope to gain from it. I had two reasons for wanting to learn Czech. Firstly, my long-term partner is Czech, and I wanted to learn his language. Secondly, at the time of my research, we had just booked to go on a three and a half month holiday to the Czech Republic once I completed my studies and so I had the perfect motivation to learn the language.

I soon discovered there are more challenges to learning a lesser spoken language such as Czech through this method. For widely spoken languages such as French, German and Spanish, it is easy to track down books in those languages. For Czech, even this basic step was extremely difficult. I planned to start reading picture books and then work my way up to reading a Czech children's novel. I searched the university library, the public library and tried a few bookstore which I knew stocked foreign language titles. No luck. I spent hours searching through multilingual bookshops online, but the only titles I could find with Czech were language dictionaries, grammar books or phrase books. Finally, I looked up the Czech word for bookshop (*knihkupectví*) and did a Google search. Immediately, a Czech bookstore popped up, and I had hundreds of Czech language books at my disposal. Including, to my delight, Czech translations of Roald Dahl's books.

My plan was to start with Czech picture books, because the pictures in such books provide additional information about the text in order to make meaning of the language. From there, I would move on to translations of Roald Dahl books. Because I am familiar with the Roald Dahl stories in English, my knowledge of the story would provide valuable context as I read through the Czech translations, helping me to make sense of the language. Finally, I would read a Czech children's novel.

The first book I read was a children's ABC book. For each letter of the alphabet there was a short verse which used words beginning with that letter. There were also pictures. With the help of nothing more than a dictionary, the pictures and the repetition in each verse, I slowly read my way from A-Z. As I read, my brain sought out patterns in the language as it tried to make sense of the text. From there, I read other children's picture books in Czech, most notably a version of Little Red Riding Hood and books from the Krtek series, a very famous Czech children's book character. Three or four times a week I spent an hour reading my way through these books, relying on my dictionary, patterns, the pictures and my knowledge of texts to assist my understanding of the language. I did not once open a grammar book. I did not look up every single word in the dictionary. I understood the stories.

By Raelke Grimmer

Learning Czech
Through Literature

Once I had read around eight children's picture books, I started on Czech translations of Roald Dahl's books. I began with *The Twits*, and the first slab of text stared at me as a wall of unrecognisable gibberish. I scanned the page for words I already knew and names of characters. Then I looked for words I recognised as verbs, given their position in the sentence. I used my dictionary to look up the verbs, as knowing the meanings of those words would give me the most help when trying to figure out what was happening in the book. I didn't look up every single word, or worry about understanding the meaning of every single word. So long as I understood the gist of the story and what was going on, that was enough.

The further I read into the book, the greater my comprehension became. I got used to the vocabulary I could expect to see, as the same words were naturally repeated again and again over the course of the book. By the end of the book, I could read for a couple of pages before I needed to look up a word. When I read the final word in *The Twits*, I was ecstatic. I couldn't believe I'd actually managed to not only read but understand and follow the story in the book, and I couldn't wait to reach for the next book, *Fantastic Mr Fox*.

I opened the first page of *Fantastic Mr Fox*, and a slab of text slapped me in the face again. I stared at the page, frustrated, as all the words swam meaninglessly in front of my eyes. I picked up my dictionary and began the process again. This time, it didn't take as long to work my way into the text and the vocabulary I could expect to find. I repeated the process again with Roald Dahl's *George's Marvellous Medicine*, before letting go of my Roald Dahl safety net.

The last text I read for my research was *Školák Kája Mařík*, another well-known Czech children's character. The book is longer and more complex than Roald Dahl, and I didn't have the added safety of knowing the story beforehand.

This book was a struggle. Instead of being slapped in the face when I opened the book, I was grabbed by the collar and pulled into a world where I understood nothing, and it felt like no one could help me find my way. Slowly, with perseverance and my trusty dictionary, I pulled myself out of the abyss into a world where I could comprehend what was going on, even if I could not explain the meaning of every single word.

The research I undertook was an extreme scenario of text-based language learning. I deliberately limited my research to works of literature in Czech, for the sole purpose of exploring their role in language learning. When I arrived in the Czech Republic, I found my comprehension of the written language was sound. I couldn't understand the spoken language as well as I could read it, but that developed over three and a half months of being surrounded by the language. And I could only speak very little of the language. But I was able to read and understand the language.

Being exposed to real examples of Czech increased my understanding of how the language works and enabled me to unravel the patterns which govern the language. Texts written with a language learner in mind are often simplified to the point where the text loses any real meaning. The texts no longer represent how the language is really used. By experiencing the Czech language as a whole instead of grammar point by grammar point, word by word, I was able to draw on my own knowledge of texts and language to make meaning of the Czech language. No, I am not equipped to explain the intricacies of Czech grammar in a lecture. But is being able to do so ever the point of language learning?

By Raelke Grimmer

Learning Czech
Through Literature

The proficiency in Czech I was able to achieve after only four months of self-study through literature texts alone indicates that had I included a wider range of texts in a variety of forms and genres, my language skills would have been even more advanced. There is a tendency to underestimate the learner in language learning classes, in particular in Australian schools. Why do we wrap our students in cotton wool and worry that immersion from day one will scare them away from language learning? In actual fact, the opposite is true. Who goes to a language class to memorise isolated words which cannot be used together to create meaningful sentences? Students become frustrated when their use of another language is limited by the present tense, or just saying their name, or asking, "How are you?" But immerse students completely in a language from day one and they will relish in the challenge of making meaning of what they are hearing.

As a bibliophile and a linguaphile, I found a language learning method which makes sense to me, and which works for me. But if you are more into surfing than reading, why not watch surf movies dubbed or subtitled in a foreign language? If you love music, scour the internet for as many songs in your target language as you can find. If you are fascinated by the universe and space exploration, seek out articles about those topics in the language you wish to learn. I would now describe myself as a bibliolinguaphile: a person who loves and collects books in foreign languages.

There is no excuse. As a language learner, take matters into your own hands. Start engaging with real texts in the target language from day one, no matter how little you understand. Persevere. You'll be surprised by how quickly the language starts making sense.

An Interview with Professor Ghil'd Zuckermann, the Prince of Lost Languages

By Elise López

Elise López was born in the Hills where trees were plentiful and skyscrapers scarce. She now lives in the suburbs with her ever-increasing library of books bursting with the knowledge of a thousand authors. During her spare time she conducts research and writes academic pieces for publication. Her areas of interest include Phraseology, Ethno-linguistics, French literature and film, and Soviet and Post-Soviet discourse. She has studied French, Spanish, German, Russian and Polish, and was taught Morse code when she was little.

Professor Ghil'ad Zuckermann, Chair of Linguistics and Endangered Languages at the University of Adelaide, is on a mission.
Fluent in eleven languages, beginner in ten more and able to
read fifty more on top of that, his love of languages has earnt him
a reputation in linguistics around the world for his work on awak-
ening 'sleeping beauties' -languages that were once considered
endangered, dormant or in some cases, extinct. Yet this is just
the beginning for Zuckermann. Coming from Israel, a place which
exemplifies the very possibility of language revival, he seeks to
create a new transdisciplinary field that will tackle all areas of language revival including education, mental health, law, linguistics,
music, architecture, dance, and theatre. "It's a huge field," he
says. "It's much more than linguistics. I believe that in the future
there will be departments of revivalistics."

When asked what drew him to linguistics, Zuckermann replied
that even as a young boy, growing up in the small town of Eilat in
Southern Israel, he loved playing with language. "I used to write
palindromic stories (stories that you could read letter by letter
from the end to the beginning and vice versa). I used to write
bilingual homophonous poems, so poems that you would read
in both Hebrew, or Israeli, and in Italian and they would make
sense simultaneously in two different languages, but with totally
different meanings. There was something in language that always
attracted me. I always thought it had a ludic, playful component.
Not an absolutely scholarly one." However, there was also the
human aspect of language that attracted him.

Zuckermann grew up in the midst of the Yom Kippur War of 1973.
"My first memory was war; rushing to the shelter at the age of
two and a half." His memories of the claustrophobic school bomb
shelter and the assassination of President Rabin were traumatic
for him and he grew up with the desire to help people. Despite

By Elise López

An Interview with Professor
Ghil'd Zuckermann, the Prince of Lost Languages

being considered a "mathematical prodigy" from a very young age, Zuckermann chose language because of the human aspect. "Einstein thought that a good mathematician is somebody who can see the relevance of every mathematical notion to reality, whereas I felt that I was more attracted to people... I always felt that, for my heart, I wanted to be closer to people and do something which is more socially beneficial."

After earning a DPhil at Oxford and completing a research fellowship at Cambridge, he published his greatest work, entitled *Israelit Safa Yafa,* or *'Israeli – A Beautiful Language'.* The book attracted a great deal of publicity by bravely arguing that the modern form of Hebrew, now spoken in Israel, should be considered a reclaimed language that differs from Ancient Hebrew, and therefore ought to be referred to as 'Israeli'. With influences from Yiddish, Russian and Polish evident in its lexicon, syntax and grammar, the reclaimed language is a richly-diverse one, cleverly constructed for everyday use in Israel. This means that the language spoken by Israelis today is not directly derived from holy writ -a concept that has caused some more passionate readers of Zuckermann's work to direct some nasty threats towards its author.

Zuckermann is now directing his efforts towards the Indigenous languages of Australia. After moving to a few different countries, he attended a conference in Sydney, where he found the views breathtaking. "When I arrived at Sydney, I couldn't believe my eyes -so beautiful! I remember thinking the vibe was similar to Tel Aviv, but there were no terror attacks and it was more beautiful; the scenery, the harbour, the cliffs. It was incredible! I was hosted by a friend. I had no idea that she was relatively wealthy. She lived on the ocean. I thought every Australian lived on the ocean and when they open the windows, they see the cliffs." After trying out Melbourne (where he described the weather as "partly sunny, mostly shite"), he moved to Brisbane, then finally settled in Adelaide, where he works with the local Barngarla people.

The Barngarla people are one of many Aboriginal tribes which were adversely affected by the colonisation of Australia. During Australia's colonisation period, there was a man named Antony Forster who said that "the native would be sooner civilised, if the language was extinct"[1].

This ideology of killing languages in Australia has led to the sad fact that in the 21st century, out of the 330 Aboriginal languages that existed prior to colonisation, only 13 (four per cent) are still living; there are 317 'sleeping beauties' in Australia, waiting to be woken. Zuckermann's plan to revive them included two main goals. "My first goal was a general universal goal: let us help revival all over the world and let us establish this comparative analysis of language revival. The second goal was to be practically working with a specific Aboriginal tribe." After analysing all the tribes in South Australia and looking at the desires, needs and available data, he found the Barngarla people, whose language became a 'sleeping beauty' in the 1960s with the death of the final speaker, Moonie Davis. Barngarla comes from the language family called Thura-Yura, which is a sub-family of the Pama-Nyungan family. Using a dictionary from 1844, written by a German missionary called Clamor Wilhelm Schürmann, and some words recorded by Luise Hercus in Canberra, Zuckermann was able to work with the Barngarla people to begin reviving a usable amount of the Barngarla language. Together, they have created neologisms to bring the language up to date with the 21st century.

---

1   Report on a public meeting of the South Australian Missionary Society in aid of the German Mission to the Aborigines, Southern Australian, 8 September 1843, p.2.

By Elise López

An Interview with Professor
Ghil'd Zuckermann, the Prince of Lost Languages

Zuckermann is closer than ever to his goal of creating an interdisciplinary field of revivalistics. This field will involve the analysis of constraints and mechanisms, whether universal or context-specific, that exist in language reclamation all over the world. "For the first time I wanted to make a science out of it, rather than just ad hoc, a revival here in Hawaii, here in Australia, here in Israel, but with no comparative insight." The field will recognise the importance of addressing issues such as native title (compensating Aboriginal people for the linguicide committed by the government), land title (compensation for loss of land during colonisation), mental health issues, and access to language education.

Zuckermann's upcoming book, entitled *Sleeping Beauties Awake: Revivalistics, Cross-Fertilization and Wellbeing*, will look at a variety of these aspects to show the diversity involved in the field of revivalistics. The book uses the revived Israeli language as a case study, arguing that it is the most successfully revived language in history, and looks at how an insight into the methodology used in this case study can help in the revival of Australian Aboriginal languages. As the title suggests, it argues the need for cross-fertilisation, or hybridity, in reviving languages; a culmination of influences and borrowings which are necessary to fill the gaps and to make languages functional in the 21st century. "The book is anti-identicality and pro-identity," Zuckermann explains. The result will still differ enough from the languages used to influence its revival; it will still carry an identity of its own. The final chapters look at important issues such as empowerment, mental health and human rights in the Aboriginal context. This holistic approach epitomises Zuckermann's ideology on revivalistics; it's not just about reclaiming a language, it's also about reclaiming a culture and being compensated for the government's actions. *Sleeping Beauties Awake* is not just

designed for linguists, but also lawyers, anthropologists, sociol-
ogists, musicologists, teachers, theatre groups and anyone with
an interest in Aboriginal affairs.

As my interview with the Prince of Lost Languages drew to an
end, I asked him what his advice would be for all those budding
linguists hoping to accomplish great things. "Study what you
enjoy the most," he said. "You never know what will come out of
it. Don't study something simply because today there is a job in
it, because you never know what will happen in twenty years. If
you study what you like, you will be good at it." He also offered
the following advice: "If your language is endangered, don't allow
it to fall asleep. And if your language is not endangered, consider helping others in linguistic need." In Australia, linguists don't
need a PhD to assist Indigenous peoples with the reclamation of
their languages. As the field of revivalistics grows, so too will the
number of opportunities in the field. So if your linguistic interests
rest in the field of revivalistics, chances are there is a community
out there waiting for your help.

By Elise López

An Interview with Professor
Ghil'd Zuckermann, the Prince of Lost Languages

No Woman
No Cry

No Woman
No Cry

by Mae Ait Bayahya

Once upon a time, Mae received an invaluable gift for her birthday: a diary. She has been writing her life down ever since. Born in the northeast of France, she moved to Morocco four years ago, where she became a journalist for a national newspaper. Too young and too curious to settle down, she moved to Australia, looking for new experiences and new stories to tell...

I was living a basic student life in France when I suddenly decided
to pursue my journey in another country. At first I thought that
I wouldn't be so far from home, just three thousand kilometres.
But I actually ended up on another planet. I was pretty bored
in my cold and rainy hometown; I was looking for sun and new
things to discover. Well, I got plenty of them.

I was a twenty year-old independent woman, used to walking
down the streets with a smile on my face. Like every girl born and
raised in Europe, I took my freedom for granted, until I moved to
a country where the streets belong to men.

I thought I knew Morocco because I have been there several
times with my family for holidays. I thought Morocco was sun,
beach, good food and cheap souvenirs -and I was all wrong.

Two weeks after I landed in Morocco with twenty years of my life
in my luggage, I was still what we gently call "a tourist". Tourists
don't really change their way of life when visiting other countries.
They hang around with their cameras, capturing every unusual practice that they can find. Wearing my favourite outfit, blue
jeans, a colourful top and a pair of sandals, I decided to go for
a walk at the seaside all by myself. Fifteen minutes later, I had the
feeling someone was following me and it wasn't just a feeling.
I turned around and saw five guys walking behind my back and
they weren't walking to admire the seaside, they were coming
after me. I got lucky that day, rescued by a taxi driver who came
out of nowhere. You could call that a happy ending. You could
say that I didn't lose anything that day because I didn't really
get hurt, except for some of my hair, which was ripped out in the
process. But the truth is, that day I lost everything because I lost
my freedom.

by Mae Ait Bayahya

No Woman
No Cry

Lassée de ma routine d'étudiante dans une Lorraine maussade et pluvieuse, j'ai soudainement décidé de m'exiler à l'étranger. A seulement trois heures d'avion de ma lorraine natal, je pensais qu'en choisissant le Maroc, je ne serais pas tant dépaysée. Au final, j'ai atterri dans une tout autre dimension. Ma ville natale ne m'a jamais particulièrement intéressée, froide et grise à en perdre le sourire, j'étais en quête de soleil et d'aventure. J'en ai eu plus qu'il n'en faut…

J'avais vingt ans, le sourire aux lèvres. J'étais comme toutes les jeunes filles de ma génération, fraîche, indépendante et déterminée. Comme toutes les jeunes filles nées dans un monde « libre », je prenais mes libertés pour acquises jusqu'à ce que j'atterrisse dans un monde où la rue appartient encore aux hommes.

Après quelques séjours passés en famille au Maroc, à me faire dorer sur la plage et à m'empiffrer de délicieux mets orientaux, je pensais tout connaître de ce pays. J'étais loin du compte.

Deux semaines après avoir atterri en terre marocaine, avec vingt ans de ma vie dans mes bagages, je n'étais encore qu'une « touriste ». Un touriste ne change pas ses habitudes. Il arpente les rues, appareil photo en main, scrutant les habitants et les pratiques locales d'un air émerveillé. Vêtue d'un jean, d'un petit top rouge et d'une paire de sandales, je n'ai pas résisté à l'idée de m'offrir une ballade le long de l'océan. Quinze minute après le début de ma ballade, j'eu la sensation d'être suivie. En me tournant discrètement, j'aperçus cinq jeunes hommes sur mes pas. Visiblement ils n'étaient pas là pour admirer la vue, j'étais devenue leur proie. Ce jour-là, la chance m'a épargné. Sauvée in extremis par un miraculeux chauffeur de taxi, vous n'aurez finalement pas besoin de mouchoirs à la lecture de ceci. On pourrait penser que je n'ai pas perdu grand chose ce jour-là, ci ce n'est quelques cheveux sauvagement arrachés. Pourtant ce jour-là, j'ai perdu mes libertés, j'ai donc tout perdu.

No Woman
No Cry

This is how I stepped out into what I like to call "the Moroccan jungle". A wild world where women have no rights but to
stay home raising the kids, cooking and watching some stupid
television programs which teach them how to be good house-
wives-such a cliché that I wouldn't believe it if I hadn't spent three
years in the country.

Moroccan society is divided into two categories: the upper class
and the lower class. The middle class doesn't exist. You have
to be rich. If not, you are poor. Of course, there is a difference
between people living in shantytown and people with a real roof
above their heads, but even if you can afford a real apartment, if
you are not rich, you are poor. Everything has a price in Morocco:
friendship, love, respect, safety, freedom and rights. And if you
are not rich, you can't afford any of this.

As a journalist, I have met a lot of people and I have been on both
sides. My wage would definitely put me in the lower class, since
I couldn't even pay the rent for my apartment by myself. But the
social life of a journalist in the arts is pretty rich. As a "friend"
of movie directors, actors, musicians and singers, I have slept
in the best palace in the country, I have attended many concerts, operas, and movie premieres. I have shared my lunches
and dinners with millionaires when my kitchen pantry was full of
one-dollar Asian noodles. But those people don't really live in
Morocco, they live in a closed bunker. In a world where everyone
knows everyone, they take their kids to private schools in their
massive cars with black windows, because they don't want to see
what is happening outside. They only go to private areas: private
pools, private beaches, private clubs and when they are bored,
they fly to Europe for a couple of weeks. In the meantime, the rest
of the population tries to survive. The thing is, when you have no
money, the only activity you can afford is hanging around in the

by Mae Ait Bayahya

No Woman
No Cry

C'est ainsi que j'ai fait mon entrée dans ce que j'aime appeler « la jungle marocaine ». Un monde barbare dans lequel les femmes n'ont d'autres droits que celui de rester à la maison pour élever les enfants, cuisiner et s'abrutir devant des programmes télévisées.

Bienvenue au Maroc où la société est divisée en deux catégories. Oubliez la classe moyenne, elle n'existe point. Au Maroc, vous êtes riche où vous êtes pauvre, vous n'avez pas d'autre option. Certes, on y trouve différents degrés de pauvreté, certains parviennent à échapper aux bidonvilles et à s'offrir un toit et des murs de brique. Quand bien même vous pouvez vous offrir un appartement digne du nom, vous n'êtes pas riche pour autant. Tout se paye au Maroc, l'amitié, l'amour, le respect, la sécurité, la liberté et les droits. Et si vous n'êtes pas riche, vous n'aurez rien de tout cela.

En tant que journaliste, j'ai fait de très nombreuses rencontres et j'ai longuement navigué entre ces deux mondes. A en juger par la misérable somme inscrite sur ma fiche de paye, j'étais bel et bien pauvre. Mais ma vie de journaliste culturelle était, quant à elle, particulièrement riche et m'offrait des avantages considérables. Amie avec des cinéastes, des acteurs, des musiciens, des chanteurs… J'ai dormi dans les plus beaux palaces marocains, j'étais présente à tous les concerts, opéras, et avant-premières, j'ai partagé mes déjeuners et mes diners presse avec des millionnaires alors qu'à la maison je devais me limiter aux nouilles instantanées. Mais tout ces gens fortunés ne vivent pas réellement au Maroc, ils vivent dans une bulle hermétique complétement coupés de la réalité. Ils vivent dans un monde où tout le monde se connaît, ils inscrivent leurs enfants à l'école privés pour qu'ils soient entourés d'enfants de même standing. Ils n'arpentent la rue qu'à bord de leurs gros cylindrés à vitre teinté pour choisir de qui ils veulent être vus et surtout pour ne voir que ce qu'ils ont envie de voir. Ils ne fréquentent que les piscines privées, les plages privées, les clubs privés

No Woman
No Cry

streets. That is exactly the reason why the streets are so dangerous. Thousands of people (men), trying to kill the day with only
a few coins in their pockets. The main activity, after petrol sniffing
and pickpocketing, is sexual harassment. After what happened
to me within the first few weeks of my stay, I stopped smiling in
the streets and I changed my entire closet. No more colourful
tops for me. Black became my favourite colour. Rule number one
of survival: be discreet, wear comfortable shoes and walk fast.
It didn't stop men from harassing me in the streets but at least
I knew that I was prepared for a race in case I had to run for my
life. And when they gave me a break, for ten or twenty minutes,
I could see some other girls being harassed. Week after week,
I had new stories to tell. One of my friends crossed the path of
a thief twice. Threatened by a knife, she had to give up her purse
with everything inside: glasses, keys, wallet, medicine, ID. Another
of my friends used to wear a beautiful gold necklace that she received as a gift from her mother. She was waiting for a cab in the
street when a biker passed by and ripped it from her neck. Rule
number two of survival: never wear anything shiny.

Every time I had to walk down the streets, I felt sick. Like most of
the Moroccan women, I was living in fear. Some places were so
dangerous that I had to ask my friends to play bodyguard. And
there is no worse feeling than feeling completely vulnerable, so
vulnerable that you have to ask your boyfriends to escort you.
One could argue that giving up on heels, skirts and jewellery is
annoying, but not dramatic. But this is much more than a dressing
issue. We are talking about freedom; freedom to walk down the
street, feeling like a human being and not like a piece of meat.

I know sexual harassment is everywhere and not only in Morocco,
but the thing is, in Morocco, there is no justice for women. Try to
go to the police and they will laugh at you and tell you that it is

by Mae Ait Bayahya

No Woman
No Cry

et lorsque tout ceci devient ennuyant à mourir, ils s'envolent pour l'Europe pour se refaire une santé. Pendant ce temps là, la population marocaine, la vraie, tente de survivre. Mais quand on n'a pas d'argent, la seule activité que l'on peut s'offrir c'est de trainer dans les rues. Et c'est ainsi que la rue se transforme en zone de danger.

Chaque jour, des milliers de jeunes marocains arpentent les rues du matin au soir et du soir au matin, avec quelques centimes en poche. Leur occupation préférée, après l'inhalation de gasoil et le pickpocket, c'est le harcèlement sexuel.

Après l'incident dont j'ai été victime au début de mon séjour, j'ai bien entendu arrêté de sourire dans les rues et j'ai entièrement refait ma garde robe. Adieux les petits hauts colorés, le noir est ainsi devenu ma couleur préférée. Règle de survie numéro un : être discrète, porter des chaussures confortables et marcher vite, très vite. Cela n'a pas empêché les marocains de m'harceler dans les rues mais au moins, j'étais préparée pour le pire. Lorsque, par chance, je n'étais pas suivie par une voiture, un piéton ou un cyclomoteur, j'assistais au harcèlement d'une de mes semblables. Semaines après semaines, les histoires et les témoignages s'agression n'en finissaient plus. Une de mes amies a croisé le chemin d'un voleur à deux reprises. Menacée par un couteau, elle s'est résignée à donner son sac à main et toutes ses fournitures. Une autre de mes amies avait l'habitude de porter une chaine en or, offerte par sa mère, autour de son cou. Alors qu'elle attendait un taxi en bas de chez elle, un homme sur un vélo le lui a arraché de son cou. Règle de survie numéro deux : ne jamais rien porter d'étincelant.

Toute les fois où j'ai du affronter la rue, j'en étais malade. Comme la plupart des femmes marocaines, je vivais dans la peur. Certains endroits étaient tellement dangereux qu'il m'était impossible d'y aller sans l'escorte de mes amis. Il n'y a pas pire sentiment que de

No Woman
No Cry

your fault -if you look too attractive, you should stay home. Yes, as unbelievable as it sounds, this is their answer, unless you have money and you are willing to pay them a lot to do their job. Then they would stay up all night to track your assailants and put them in jail for money, but only for money. I guess if you have no money, you are not worth it. This is how "money" became the ultimate goal for the majority of Moroccan women. They know that with money they will have respect, dignity and freedom. But when you come from the "jungle", you have no chance to get a decent wage and a good job. No matter if you are a genius or not, with no money or no friends in high places, you will never make it to the recruiter's office. So is there any chance for Moroccan women to get their freedom? Yes, by marrying an old and rich man. Cliché again, but true. Sadly, that's the reason I have watched many of my girlfriends marry forty-five year-old men. At first, I was very judgmental about their decision to do so. For me, love could never be forced or motivated to marry by anything other than true love. In Morocco they called me naïve. I have realised that for some women, love is a way out, a second chance for a decent life. At first I was really disappointed that my friends were choosing what I used to call "the easiest option", instead of fighting for their rights. But now I think they are actually extremely brave to have sacrificed love for safety and dignity. One of my friends once told me "Mae, what do you want me to do? I have no way out but marriage. I can't afford a car with my wage, I can't afford a life in private clubs, private beaches, I can't afford safety and I don't want to live like this. But I have met this guy, he is old but he has money and my life would be so much better by his side." What can I say to that?

Of course men know that. They know that with money they will have all the girls that they want so, of course, they take advantage of the situation. The thing is, the situation won't get better after

by Mae Ait Bayahya

No Woman
No Cry

se sentir vulnérable, vulnérable au point de devoir recourir à une présence masculine. Dans quel monde étais-je….

Je vous l'accorde, renoncer à ses talons hauts, ses jupes et ses bijoux peut être ennuyant mais ça n'a rien de dramatique. Mais tout cela va bien plus loin qu'un code vestimentaire. La femme marocaine a renoncé à ses droits et libertés. A la liberté de marcher dans la rue tel un être humain et non tel un vulgaire morceau de viande. Je sais que le harcèlement sexuel sévit partout dans le monde mais au Maroc, les femmes sont les oubliées de la justice. Essayez un jour d'aller au commissariat pour dénoncer un viol ou une agression, ils vous riront au nez et vous diront que c'est de votre faute, que votre place est à la maison. Cette réponse, c'est la seule chose que vous obtiendrez d'eux, à moins que vous ayez de l'argent et que vous soyez prêts à payer cher pour que justice soit faite. Mais si vous n'avez pas d'argent, vous n'avez pas de justice.

C'est ainsi que « l'argent » devint la priorité absolue des femmes marocaines, conscientes qu'avec de l'argent, elles auront droit au respect, la dignité et à la liberté. Mais lorsqu'on vient de la « jungle », on n'a aucune chance d'obtenir un emploi décent et un salaire raisonnable. Qu'importe l'intelligence ou le talent, sans argent et donc sans amis haut placés, vous n'aurez rien. Quelles chances ont donc les marocaines de pouvoir acquérir leurs libertés? Le mariage avec un sexagénaire plein aux as. Tellement cliché mais tellement vrai!

C'est ainsi que j'ai tristement contemplé mes amies se marier avec des hommes de vingt ou trente ans leur ainé. Au départ cela m'insupportait. J'étais très dure envers mes amies, je les ai sévèrement jugé sur leur comportement que je qualifiais de « malhonnête ». Je fais partie de celles qui croient en l'amour et en sa sincérité. Au Maroc on appelle ça « être naïve ». Puis, j'ai réalisé que pour

No Woman
No Cry

the Arab Spring. Even if the situation in Morocco wasn't as bad as
the situation in Tunisia and Egypt, the prime minister, Abdel-Ilah
Benkiran, leader of the "Justice and Development Party" doesn't
really fight for justice. He fights for Islamism and conservatism,
and his ideas about how women should spend their time make
me sick. When women are desperately expecting the mentality
to evolve, Benkiran deeply encourages women to stay home to
raise their kids and take care of their husbands. The truth is, the
only things evolving in Morocco are the facilities. They are trying
to create a mini Dubai with big towers, metro airlines, malls… but
they want to stop society from evolving. All the money goes into
facilities when thousands of kids are kept away from school.

School provides education and knowledge and with knowledge,
citizens will fight for their rights and rise against machismo and
conservatism, but the government doesn't want that to happen.
Keeping the education system weak is a way for them to control
the minds of citizens and it works -guess who made this guy
prime minister.

It took me three years to realize how lucky I was to have that
damn red passport, my way out of there. For the first time in my
life, I felt blessed for being born in my cold and rainy Lorraine.
To be honest, through these three years, I had tons of reasons
to leave every day. I could have terminated my stay much earlier.
My family couldn't understand why I was inflicting that on myself
when I could simply go back to them. Why did I stay? Because
when you are young, innocent and naïve you think that you can
fix everything and save the world. Until you grow up and realize
that the only thing you can fix is yourself. This though life affected
me more than it should have. I was completely damaged from the
inside. My brain was tired. Until the day my own reflection in the
mirror scared me. I couldn't recognize myself anymore. My world

by Mae Ait Bayahya

No Woman
No Cry

beaucoup de femmes, le mariage était une échappatoire, une chance pour une vie meilleure. J'ai souvent été déçue de voir mes amies choisir le mariage comme porte de secours au lieu de se battre dignement pour leurs droits. Mais avec le recul, je leur tire mon chapeau pour être capable de sacrifier le véritable amour au nom de la sécurité et de la dignité.

Un jour une amie m'a dit, « Mae, que voudrais-tu que je fasse ? Je n'ai d'autre solution que le mariage. Je n'aurais jamais les moyens de me payer une voiture, de fréquenter les clubs privés, les plages privés… Je n'aurais jamais les moyens d'être en sécurité et je ne veux pas passer ma vie ainsi. J'ai rencontré cet homme, il est vieux mais il a de l'argent et ma vie va complètement changer à ses côtés. » Que puis-je répondre à cela ?

Bien sur, les hommes ont conscience de cette fatalité. Ils savent qu'avec de l'argent, ils auront toutes les filles qu'ils veulent et ils profitent donc de cette situation.

Le pire dans tout cela c'est que les choses ne vont pas en s'améliorant. Depuis le printemps arabe, la situation s'aggrave. Bien que le Maroc n'ait pas subi ce qu'à subi l'Egypte ou la Tunisie, le premier Ministre marocain, j'ai nommé Abdel-Ilah Benkiran, leader du parti politique « Justice et développement » ne se souci guère de la justice. Ses préoccupations s'orientent davantage vers le retour à un Maroc conservateur et islamique. Ses idées sur le comportement des femmes marocaines sont à vomir. Alors qu'elles sont de plus en plus nombreuses à espérer un changement des mentalités, Benkiran encourage les femmes à rester à la maison pour élever leurs enfants et prendre soin de leur époux. Triste constat : la seule chose qui évolue au Maroc ce sont les infrastructures. Tramway, métro aérien, TGV, centre commerciaux à l'américaine, c'est bien connu, les hommes et les machines… Le Maroc s'enrichi matériellement et s'appauvrit intellectuellement.

No Woman
No Cry

was dark and I was down the edge. I still remember how badly
I needed to sleep to give my soul a break. So yes, I did run away
to fix myself, before it was too late. I realized I wasn't the person
I wanted to be and it wasn't the life I wanted to live. I escaped
from the darkness. I had to do it for myself and for all these
Moroccan women who would kill to be in my shoes

by Mae Ait Bayahya

No Woman
No Cry

La moindre parcelle de terrain se vend à une somme astronomique sur le marché international alors que dans certains villages, les enfants attendent encore qu'on leur construise une école. L'école procure éducation et savoir et avec le savoir, les citoyens auront les ressources nécessaires pour réclamer leurs droits et se soulever contre le machisme et le conservatisme. Le gouvernement en a conscience et c'est précisément pour cela qu'il maintient le système scolaire au plus bas niveau. Priver les gens de savoir c'est les priver de pouvoir.

Il m'a fallu trois ans pour réaliser à quel point j'étais chanceuse d'avoir ce foutu passeport rouge, mon passe pour la liberté. Pour la première fois de ma vie, je me suis sentie bénie d'être née en Lorraine, même si froide et pluvieuse. Pour être totalement honnête, au cours de ces trois ans, la vie me donnait chaque jour mile et unes raisons de tout quitter. J'aurais pu partir bien avant, d'ailleurs ma famille n'a jamais compris pourquoi je m'infligeais tant de peine au lieu de tout simplement rentrer auprès d'eux. Pourquoi suis-je resté ? Car lorsqu'on est jeune, innocente et naïve, on pense que l'on peut tout réparer et que l'on peut sauver le monde. Jusqu'à ce que l'on grandisse et réalise que la seule chose que l'on peut réparer c'est soi-même. Cette vie à la dur m'a affecté bien plus qu'elle n'aurait du. J'étais complétement détruite de l'intérieur. Mon cerveau était épuisé. Jusqu'au jour où j'ai été effrayée par mon propre reflet dans le miroir, je n'étais plus moi-même. Mon monde était sombre et j'étais au bord du gouffre. Seul le sommeil apaisait mon âme, je m'en souviens comme si c'était hier. Oui, j'ai pris la fuite pour m'auto-réparer avant qu'il ne soit trop tard. J'ai réalisé que je n'étais pas la personne que je voulais être et que ce n'était pas la vie que je voulais vivre. Je me suis échappé des ténèbres. Je devais le faire pour moi-même et pour toutes ces femmes marocaines qui tueraient pour être à ma place.

No Woman
No Cry

Barossa German: Recording and Renewing Heritage

by Dr. Peter Mickan

Dr. Peter Mickan is a senior researcher in the Discipline of Linguistics, University of Adelaide, South Australia. He conducts and supervises research on academic literacy, text-based curriculum design and language learning. His 2013 book *Language Curriculum Design and Socialisation*, Bristol, Multilingual Matters, sets out the principles and practice of text-based teaching based on social semiotics theory of language and learning is based on Halliday's (1978) social theory and language as a social semiotic.

German speaking immigrants settled the Barossa and regional South Australia in the mid-19th century. In the decades following the establishment of the colony of South Australia in 1836, German migration from central Europe flourished due to political conflict, religious dissension, economic upheaval and natural disasters in their homelands. The settlers sought security, liberty, land, and religious freedom from state dictates. They were welcomed by the English-speaking settlers. My parents were born in 1913 and read and spoke German when they were ninety years old. Unfortunately we did not speak German at home, a common experience of language loss for my generation.

In the First and Second World Wars, when Australia was militarily aligned with Britain against Germany and its allies, the public use of German was suppressed. During the First World War the South Australian parliament passed legislation to close eighty German medium schools. During both wars German speakers were maligned publicly and privately, and some community leaders, including Lutheran pastors, were interned. The German names of towns and villages were changed to English names. In the thirty years from 1916 to 1946, the negative attitudes and governmental legislation undermined the public use of German in the community. This had the effect of discouraging the private use of German. Even within families, parents no longer spoke German with their children. After the Second World War German was taught as a foreign language in public schools, not as a community language. People's use of German for public events such as church services was curtailed with few congregations continuing German worship services for special religious festivals. Today German has disappeared from public use in the community, representing a diminution of culture and of heritage.

by Dr. Peter Mickan

Barossa German:
Recording and Renewing Heritage

In the Barossa Valley, German was the community language for social, business, education and cultural purposes. The Lutheran communities built churches, established German schools and colleges, and conducted religious and social activities in German. However, the impact of two World Wars and dominance of English resulted in the dramatic retraction of German from the middle of the twentieth century. Children were warned not to speak German, schools teaching in German were closed by government decree in 1917, German-speaking citizens were incarcerated and German place names were eliminated. Remarkably, a few descendants from the nineteenth century immigrants have retained the ability to use German for different functions and in different domains. In fact, they identify closely with the German language. But how have elderly speakers retained their capacity to express themselves in German and to understand German in an English-speaking culture?

The immigrants to the Barossa and to other regions settled in farming communities where German was used for communal activities. They conversed in German with families and neighbours and in their day-to-day business. They not only had language in common they also shared religious beliefs. The members of the community were committed Christians. Their beliefs were based on Lutheran confessions. In their personal lives, in the privacy of their homes, they prayed in German and conducted devotions in German. They built churches as centres of community events. In the Barossa Valley and other regions the churches are physical evidence of the central place of Lutheran confessions in people's lives.

Pastors preached in German. Weddings and religious celebrations were held in German. Sunday school, confirmation lessons and meetings were conducted in German. Education was valued and church communities established schools. Teachers taught in German and in English in the parish schools.

Together with PhD student Kateryna Katsman and German col-
league Claudia Riehl I have been recording speakers who have
retained the capacity to speak German even though they are fifth
and sixth generation Australians. We have been recording elderly
speakers of German who recount learning German from parents
and grandparents. They refer in particular to religious lessons
in German for confirmation and for Sunday school. For many
settlers, German continued as the language for engaging in business, and for participation in educational and cultural practices
until the middle of the twentieth century.

During interviews they recalled bitter experiences of abuse as
children of German speakers. They explained that their parents
discouraged them from speaking German outside the home.
As we conversed, they expressed pleasure in speaking German
again, talking about their lives and families and work. We joined in
their prayers and hymn singing. In particular, they expressed the
wish to talk together in German again, and to sing and pray. Community support for German has motivated us to set up a program
for maintenance and revival of German together.

The program of German language revival is a distinctive feature
of the Barossa German project. Linguists documenting language
in communities like the Barossa, where a language has been
maintained over generations, focus on linguistic differences
from a standard language. The focus is on speakers' deficits or
mistakes or on regional varieties. Our recordings show speakers
are able to express themselves on many topics and even though
there are variations from standard German, a natural phenomenon of language change in such contexts, these do not inter-
fere with our conversations and recordings. The term 'Barossa
German' is often associated with poor grammar and a muddle of
English and German. The latter is referred to as code-switching,

by Dr. Peter Mickan

Barossa German:
Recording and Renewing Heritage

which is a common feature where two or more languages are in use. However, as a result, people speak negatively of Barossa German. We have found that the influence of sermons, confirmation lessons, Sunday school classes and access to publications maintained people's capability in German over generations and provide reasons for respecting the heritage.

We have used the term Barossa Deutsch (German) to signify a region in South Australia settled by German immigrants in which German was spoken widely until the second half of the twentieth century. The term does not identify a variety of German. The Barossa is the region and the cultural and situational context for our study. The documentation of Barossa German provides insights into community members' German use and maintenance. This is the resource which has influenced our revival program. The general intention is through documentation and analysis of German to contribute to revival of German amongst community members through valuing German language heritage and honouring German speakers who are descendants of the mid-nineteenth century immigrants.

Once a month in 2014, and continuing in 2015, German speakers and those who wish to speak or improve their German have gathered over Kaffee und Kuchen (coffee and cake). We read, discuss, plan and sing in German. The community response has been overwhelming. The community is now working to renew German use and to support the teaching of German in schools. A parent group is planning to establish a German language school where their children will be able to speak and read in German. These developments are the next chapter in the documentation and revival of German in the Barossa and other regions in South Australia.

Revealing the History, Digging Etymology

Menguak Sejarah, Menggali Etimologi

by Ahmad Junaidi

Ahmad Junaidi is a native Indonesian speaker. He mostly speaks in an accent influenced by the Sasak language, his mother tongue spoken on Lombok Island (that less popular island next to Bali). He graduated from the University of Adelaide with a Master of Arts in Applied Linguistics and he is now an English teacher at the University of Mataram and a volunteer at the Jage Kastare Foundation, a community learning centre promoting literacy development, English learning, cultural preservation and arts appreciation for kids and teenagers at Ungge Village, Central Lombok.

Every word in this essay, as you're reading this essay and now looking at THIS word, including the dots and marks among them, has its own history. Each of them has been through decades and centuries that have slightly or drastically changed its meaning. If understanding the history of Homo sapiens is important, it is also important to know the history of their communication elements. This essay sets out the history or etymology of words, the importance of etymology to reveal the history of human experience embedded in the language, and how learning etymology can help foreign language learners to better learn the target language they're learning.

Knowing the history of a word equals studying a part of the history of mankind. The word 'narcissistic' as we know it has a negative sense in the first place before it is now becoming more and more accepted in Indonesia and is viewed as merely a normal behaviour of a sub-culture, as in the phrase 'anak narsis'. Being called 'narsis' in the Indonesian language (which translates to 'narcissist' in English) is very common among Indonesian urban youth although in its original meaning this word is not as casual as it is now. Indonesian speakers adopted this word from the English 'narcissist' which means 'someone who loves himself excessively and tends to be selfish'. Its origin is from a term used by a community of psychoanalysts in Germany to describe a psychological condition of 'narzissismus' which was then used by the same circle of professionals in the UK and altered into the word 'narcissism'. The question is, how did they come up with the word? There's a reason for sure. In the mythology of Ancient Greek, we know Narcissus, a handsome hunter who was condemned by the river fairy and was romantically rejected, who spent the rest of his life staring at his own reflection on the surface of the pond with a strong feeling of admiration and love for himself. Experts then used the mythology to name the emotional phenomenon.

by Ahmad Junaidi

Revealing the History,
Digging Etymology

Setiap kata dalam esai ini, termasuk kata INI, termasuk juga tanda baca yang ada di antara kata-kata tersebut, memiliki sejarahnya sendiri. Setiap kata tersebut telah melalui rentang waktu yang panjang yang sedikit maupun banyak telah mengubah maknanya. Tulisan ini mengemukakan tentang sejarah atau asal muasal kata atau etimologi, pentingnya etimologi untuk memaknai ulang sejarah dan pengalaman manusia yang tertanam dalam bahasa, dan juga pada bagian akhir akan menggambarkan bagaimana etimologi dapat membantu pembelajar bahasa asing dalam mempelajari dan mengenal bahasa yang dipelajarinya.

Mengetahui sejarah dari mana sebuah kata berasal adalah seperti mempelajari bagian dari sejarah perjalanan manusia. Kata 'narsis' yang kita kenal sekarang memiliki makna yang dulu mutlak negatif sebelum sekarang menjadi lebih diterima dan hanya dilihat sebagai perilaku sebuah sub-kultur, 'anak narsis'. Menjadi narsis adalah hal biasa, sedangkan dalam makna asalnya kata ini tidaklah sebiasa itu. Penutur Bahasa Indonesia mengadopsi kata ini dari Bahasa Inggris 'narcist' yang berarti seseorang yang hanya mencintai dirinya sendiri secara berlebihan dan cenderung egois. Kata ini sebelumnya adalah kata yang berasal dari lingkar ahli psikoanalisa di Jerman untuk menggambarkan sebuah kondisi psikologis 'narzissismus' yang kemudian dipakai oleh lingkar profesi yang sama di Inggris dengan kata 'narcissism'. Lalu darimana para psikoanalis ini bisa memakai kata ini? Tentu ada alasannya. Mitologi Yunani Kuno tentang Narcissus, pemburu tampan yang karena dikutuk oleh peri sungai yang ditolaknya menghabiskan sisa hidupnya memandangi bayangannya di permukaan kolam dengan penuh kekaguman dan rasa cinta. Para ahli itupun menggunakan tokoh dalam mitologi ini untuk menamai fenomena tersebut, lalu dari mana akar nama Narcissus? Disinilah cerita terputus. R.S.P. Bleekes mengklaim bahwa tidak jelas darimana nama ini berasal. Yang jelas adalah bahwa akhiran –sus berasal dari Bahasa Yunani

The question does not stop here. Where did the name 'Narcissus' come from? How was that poor mythological guy named? The only piece of information R.S.P. Bleekes claimed is that it is not clear where the name was derived from. What is clear is that the -sus suffix comes from the proto Greek, which does not really explain anything. To this end, we give up. No records older than the mythology texts are avaliable. The bright side, however, is that we know that 'narcissistic' was and is still used to denote a psychiatric condition.

A word that brings several elements can have more than one story because each of the elements brings a different story. The English word 'assassin' was derived from the term to name the secret Ismaili sect of Islam under the leadership of Hasan Ibn al-Sabbah who dedicated their life to kill the Christian soldiers in the crusade. Murder is usually committed after smoking the sap of marijuana or 'hashish' that ultimately made them famous as hashish smokers or 'hashisiyyin' in Arabic. Hashisiyyin. Assasin.

The word 'karantina' in Indonesian was adapted from 'quarantine' in English, which has French roots of 'quarante' and '-aine' which when combined mean 'about forty days', i.e. the length of time a ship and its crew suspected of bearing infectious diseases should be retained in dock before making contact in the harbor.

'Alpukat', 'Avocado', still in Indonesian, can be traced back to Aztec's 'ahuacatl' which means 'testicles (scrotum)'. In addition to the testicles-resembling shape, the avocado is also often used as an 'aphrodisiac', a food that triggers sexual arousal.

The word 'minggu' in Indonesian was derived from the word 'domingo', a Portuguese, Spanish and popular Christian name. It is a special name because the names of the other days in Indone-

by Ahmad Junaidi

Revealing the History,
Digging Etymology

proto. Sampai di sini kita menyerah. Tidak ada catatan yang lebih tua daripada naskah mitologi itu. Sisi baiknya adalah kita mengetahui bahwa 'narsis' sebelumnya adalah suatu kondisi kejiwaan.

Setiap kata yang kita pakai sekarang memiliki ceritanya sendiri yang kadang mengagetkan. Bahkan satu kata bisa memiliki lebih dari satu cerita dikarenakan elemennya membawa cerita berbeda. Kata Bahasa Inggris 'assasin' berasal dari istilah untuk menamai sekte Islam rahasia Ismaili di bawah pimpinan Hasan Ibnu Al-Sabbah yang hidupnya didedikasikan untuk membunuh tentara kristen di perang salib. Pembunuhan ini biasa dilakukan setelah menghisap hashish atau getah ganja yang akhirnya membuat mereka dikenal dengan nama penghisap hashish atau 'hashisiyyin' dalam Bahasa Arab. Assasin. Penghisap hashish.

Karantina dalam bahasa Indonesia diambil dari 'quarantine' dalam bahasa Inggris yang memiliki akar bahasa Perancis 'quarante' dan '-aine' yang jika digabungkan memiliki makna 'sekitar empat puluh hari', yaitu lama sebuah kapal dan kru yang dicurigai mengidap penyakit menular harus ditahan di dermaga sebelum melakukan kontak di pelabuhan.

'Alpukat', masih dalam bahasa Indonesia, memiliki pangkal bahasa Aztec 'ahuacatl' yang berarti buah pelir (scrotum). Selain bentuknya yang mirip buah pelir, alpukat juga seringkali digunakan 'aphrodisiac', pemicu gairah seksual.

Kata 'minggu' berasal dari kata 'domingo', Bahasa Portugis dan Spanyol yang dekat dengan istilah keagamaan atau tokoh dalam agama Kristen. Hal ini spesial karena nama-nama hari lain dalam Bahasa Indonesia yaitu Senin, Selasa, Rabu, Kamis, Jumat berasal dari Bahasa Arab. Banyak penceramah kemudian 'melarang' pemeluk agama Islam menggunakan kata 'minggu', akibat sian i.e. Senin, Selasa, Rabu, Kamis, Jumat and Sabtu were taken from the Arabic. Many religious traditionalists then 'prohibit' Muslims to use the word 'Minggu' because it was a term from another religious group. They suggest 'Ahad', another word derived from the Arabic, the language of the Quran .

Ten in 10 random Indonesians do not know why they were called Indonesians. So, here is what should be in the school curriculum. In 1847, an ethnologist of a journal in Singapore, George Samuel Windsor Earl wrote that the population of the occupied Dutch East Indies should have a unique name to refer to their occupied territory without having to be obedient when called 'Nederlands (ch) -Indië'. He then proposed the European misnomer given to any areas stretching along Persia to China as 'India', he proposed the name 'indunesia' or 'malayunesia' (nesos > nesia, Greek for island or archipelago) He himself then chose 'malayunesia' and dropped the word 'indunesia' because it was considered more appropriate to the race of the inhabitants. Also 'indunesia' etymologically could have also been used to refer to other islands such as the Maldives and Sri Lanka, which are also located near the East Indies, India. However, other scholars then took the word 'Indunesia' because this word was already very familiar in Europe who called these islands 'Indies'. The name was then used by Ki Hajar Dewantara and became our official name.

The Indonesian archipelago is home to hundreds of Indigenous languages. These languages have their own system which have formed over a long time and has evolved since then. Some words in these languages died, and some were born. To give an idea of the word variation in these languages, here are some words from several different tribes in Indonesia for the word 'sea'.

by Ahmad Junaidi

Revealing the History,
Digging Etymology

terlalu identik dengan salah satu agama lain, dan menggantinya dengan 'ahad', kata yang berasal dari Bahasa Arab, bangsa yang melahirkan Islam.

Sepuluh dari sepuluh orang Indonesia tidak mengetahui sejarah penamaan negerinya sendiri. Berikut adalah sepotong informasi yang seharusnya ada dalam kurikulum sekolah. Pada 1847, ahli etnologi sebuah jurnal di Singapura, George Samuel Windsor Earl menulis bahwa penduduk terjajah Hindia-Belanda seharusnya memiliki nama yang khas untuk menyebut wilayahnya. Bukan manut saja dipanggil 'Nederlands(ch)-Indië'. Berdasar pada misnomer orang Eropa yang menyebut semua wilayah yang terbentang dari Persia sampai Cina sebagai 'India', ia mengajukan nama 'indunesia' atau 'malayunesia' (nesos > nesia, Bahasa Yunani untuk pulau atau kepulauan) Dia sendiri kemudian memilih 'malayunesia' dan membuang kata 'indunesia' karena dianggap lebih sesuai dengan ras penghuninya. Sementara 'indunesia' bisa saja digunakan untuk menyebut kepulauan lain seperi Maladewa dan Srilangka yang memang berada di dekat Hindia, India. Akan tetapi, ahli lain kemudian mengambil kata 'indunesia' ini karena dianggap sudah terlanjur akrab di Eropa yang biasa menyebut kepulauan ini 'Indische'. Nama yang kemudian dipakai oleh Ki Hajar Dewantara dan kemudian menjadi nama kita sampai dengan sekarang.

Kepulauan Indonesia merupakan tempat berkembangnya ratusan bahasa daerah. Bahasa-bahasa ini memiliki sistem sendiri yang terbentuk dalam waktu yang panjang dan mengalami evolusi. Kata-kata dalam bahasa tersebut ada yang mati dan ada yang terlahir. Ada yang hanya berumur sebentar saja. Untuk memberikan gambaran tentang variasi bahasa, berikut adalah beberapa kata dari beberapa suku berbeda di Indonesia untuk kata 'laut'.

Batak Karo language on Sumatra island → lawit
Makassar language in Sulawesi → tamparang
Java language in Java → segoro
Minang language in Sumatra → lauik
Rima language on Sumbawa Island → moti
Sasak in Lombok Island → segara
Pujut dialect of Sasal language → mare

What thought comes to your mind when you know that one of
the Romance languages, Italian, has the same word for 'sea',
i.e 'mare', the same word for 'sea' in the Teruwai sub dialect
(a sub of the Pujut dialect, one of the four dialects in the Sasak
language, an Indigeneous language on Lombok Island, Indonesia). It should be noted that the word 'mare' is not used in other
areas on Lombok Island, and is only used in the Southern beach
area. Is this a coincidence? Does the similarity in four sequenc-
es of sound have nothing to do whatsoever with the meaning?
I would argue that the word 'goreng' in the Teruwai sub-dialect
which means 'dirty' in Indonesian has nothing to do with the word
'goreng' in the Indonesian language which means 'to fry'. It is safe
to say that this is a coincidence because the meaning is far too
different. Could we do the same to the 'mare' case? Two words.
Same sound combination, same meaning. Both the words 'mare'
have the same meaning of 'sea'. I would not associate the word
'mare' /me/ in Italian with 'mare' /mare/ in the Sasak language
because they have distinct meanings and different pronuncia-
tions. However, I'm intrigued to find the answer as to why these
two languages have the same word for 'sea'. In a previous article
about the etymology of the Indonesian third person 'dia', we
found the answer to where this word came from. That the word
'dia' didn't just get there randomly, that the word 'dia' has a long
history. As it is used widely, it can be searched and investigated.

by Ahmad Junaidi

Revealing the History,
Digging Etymology

Bahasa Batak Karo di Sumatra → lawit
Bahasa Makassar di Sulawesi → tamparang
Bahasa Jawa di Pulau Jawa → segoro
Bahasa Minang di Sumatra → lauik
Bahasa Bima di Pulau Sumbawa → moti
Bahasa Sasak di Pulau Lombok → segare
Bahasa Sasak dialek pujuk, sub-dialek Teruwai → mare

Apa yang kamu pikirkan ketika ternyata salah satu bahasa Roman, yaitu Bahasa Italia memiliki kata yang sama untuk 'laut' yaitu 'mare'? Kata yang sama dengan kata untuk 'laut' dalam Bahasa Sasak dialek Pujut, sub dialek Teruwai, salah satu satu sub-dialek dari salah satu dari empat dialek di salah satu bahasa Sasak yang notabene berpenutur kecil di rumpun keluarga bahasa Austronesia di Nusantara. Perlu dicatat bahwa kata 'mare' tidak dipakai di daerah tutur Sasak lain di Pulau Lombok, dan hanya dipakai di daerah pantai Selatan. Sebuah kebetulankah? Apakah kesamaan kombinasi empat bunyi yang hampir sama persis ini tak memiliki kaitan apapun seperti kasus kata 'goreng' dalam Bahasa Sasak sub-dialek Teruwai yang berarti 'kotor' dalam Bahasa Indonesia? Kita bisa saja berpendapat demikian akan tetapi ini adalah jawaban yang 'malas. Kedua kata 'mare' ini memiliki makna sama. Laut. Saya tidak akan mengaitkan kata 'mare' dalam Bahasa Inggris dengan 'mare' dalam Bahasa Sasak karena memang maknanya berbeda dan pelafalannnya berbeda. Dalam tulisan sebelumnya tentang etimologi kata ganti orang ketiga, para ahli menemukan jawaban dari mana kata 'dia' berasal. Bahwa kata 'dia' tidak secara acak muncul begitu saja. Bahwa kata 'dia' memiliki sejarah panjang yang karena kata ini dipakai luas, dapat dicari dan kemudian diteliti. Para ahli dapat menemukan darimana kata ini berasal karena kata ini dianggap penting. Tentu memang kata 'mare' di sub dialek Pujut, Bahasa Sasak tidak sepopuler kata 'dia' dalam Bahasa Indonesia. Akan

The experts could find out where this word originated because this word is considered important and popular. Certainly the word 'mare' in the Sasak language is not as popular as the word for 'he or she' in Indonesian. However, the fact that they posit a strong similarity may tell us something about the history of these two far separated areas which probably is interesting and important for us to know.

Some of the examples above clearly illustrate that words do tell us a lot about the history of mankind and the story of their life experience. Science. One word was born somewhere on the history timeline then evolved in meaning. Studying the etymology is important because etymology is a reminder of the nature of language. Language is dynamic and is a vehicle for human history. Language learners at a more advanced level can easily guess the meaning when in a newspaper they find the word 'Amerikofilia' if prior to that they have already understood the elements that make up the word 'paedophile'. Reflective learners, with sensitive knowledge about the history of words understand that any '-phile' at the end of a word means 'the lovers of the + word it is attached to'. It is most often a wrong kind of love, as it is often used to denote a sexual or emotional disorder.

The answer to the question of why the Italian 'mare' is identical in meaning to the word from the Pujut dialect of the Sasak language 'mare' is so far unclear. Tell me it is a coincidence. People from southern Europe and people from southern Lombok, Indonesia, use the same word to denote the same object. At the moment, I don't know that yet. Neither did R.S.P. Bleekes who gave up explaining the name etymology of Narcissus. There wasn't enough data on these cases. There were probably some Italians who were spending time on vacation and started screaming 'mare' every

by Ahmad Junaidi

Revealing the History,
Digging Etymology

tetapi fakta kesamaan di atas mungkin menceritakan sesuatu tentang sejarah di masa lalu yang amat sangat menarik dan penting untuk kita ketahui.

Beberapa contoh di atas memberi gambaran jelas bahwa kata-kata bercerita tentang sejarah manusia dan cerita kehidupan yang mereka alami. Tentang ilmu pengetahuan. Sebuah kata tentu saja muncul di satu titik waktu. Kemudian berevolusi dalam makna. Mempelajari etimologi kemudian penting karena etimologi adalah pengingat tentang hakikat bahasa. Bahasa bersifat dinamis dan merupakan kendaraan bagi sejarah manusia. Pembelajar bahasa pada tingkatan yang lebih mahir bisa dengan mudah menebak makna ketika dalam sebuah koran menemukan kata 'Amerikofilia;, jika sebelumnya dia memahami elemen yang membentuk kata 'pedofilia'. Bahwa kemudian pembelajar yang reflektif terhadap proses derivasi dapat memahami bahwa sebagian besar bentuk kecintaan (yang kadang tidak wajar) terhadap sesuatu dapat disematkan kata –filia (bahasa Inggris –philia) dibelakangnya. Mereka yang reflektif terhadap etimologi, khususnya terhadap kata-kata yang populer, memiliki pemahaman yang lebih luas daripada mereka yang menghapal satu kata tidak dengan memahami elemennya. Mereka memiliki pemahaman akan sejarah di belakang kata tersebut sehingga dapat memprediksi kata lain yang memiliki elemen sama dengan kata yang telah dipelajarinya.

Jawaban untuk pertanyaan kenapa bahasa Italia 'mare' yang berarti 'laut' memiliki kata yang sama dengan 'mare' dalam Bahasa Sasak Dialek Pujut yang juga berarti laut sampai sejauh ini tidak jelas jawabannya. Silahkan saja berasumsi ini Cuma kebetulan. Orang-orang Eropa Selatan memiliki kata yang persis sama untuk menyebut hal yang sama dengan penduduk beberapa desa di pantai selatan Lombok. Sampai sejauh ini kita tidak tahu kenapa. Sama sepeti R.S.P Bleekes yang menyerah menjelaskan darimana kata time they saw the 'sea' or maybe an Italian voyager once visited the island a long time ago. We don't know. One sure thing is that some words happen to still have their traces. These traces are to be revealed and studied. They tell us about our ancestors. They want us to reveal their stories, unveiling the history by studying the etymology.

Revealing the History,
Digging Etymology

Narcissus berasal. Tidak banyak data disini yang tersedia. Mungkin saja dulu banyak pelancong dari Italia yang selalu berteriak 'mare' setiap kali melihat laut atau mungkin juga beratus tahun yang lalu ada seorang pelaut Italia yang mengunjungi pulau ini. Kita tidak tahu. Yang pasti adalaha banyak kata yang kebetulan masih memiliki cerita. Jejak informasi. Jejak-jejak ini yang harus kita kuak dan pelajari. Kata-kata ini bercerita sesuatu tentang pengalaman hidup pendahulu-pendahulu kita. Kata-kata ini menginginkan kita untuk menguak sejarah dengan mempelajari etimologi.

Menguak Sejarah,
Menggali Etimologi